BILLY PITT
HAD THEM BUILT

To Sue

Billy Pitt had them built, Buck Mulligan said, when the French were on the sea.

James Joyce *Ulysses* ('Telemachus')

BILLY PITT
HAD THEM BUILT

NAPOLEONIC TOWERS IN IRELAND

Bill Clements

The
Holliwell
Press

First published in Great Britain in 2013 by
The Holliwell Press

8 Rock Terrace
Scotgate
Stamford
Lincolnshire
PE9 2YJ

ISBN 978-0-9926104-0-1

A CIP catalogue record for this book is available from the British Library

Book designed by Stephen Dent

CONTENTS

About the Author 6

Author's Foreword 7

Introduction 8

Chapter 1   The Bantry Towers 18

Chapter 2   The Dublin Towers 32

Chapter 3   The Towers of Lough Swilly and Lough Foyle 49

Chapter 4   The Galway and Shannon Towers 66

Chapter 5   The Wexford and Louth Towers 74

Chapter 6   The Cork Towers 80

Chapter 7   The Quadrangular Towers and Signal Towers 87

            Conclusion 105

Annex A   Martello Towers Location and Description 107

Annex B   Circular Redoubts and Quadrangular Towers 111

Annex C   Irish Signal Towers and Stations 113

            Notes 116

            Bibliography 118

            Glossary 119

            Index 121

ABOUT THE AUTHOR

Bill Clements was born and educated in Northern Ireland, studying Law at the Queen's University of Belfast. In 1958 he was commissioned into the Royal Ulster Rifles (TA) and subsequently became a regular officer serving with the Royal Ulster Rifles and commanding the 1st Battalion The Royal Irish Rangers. His interest in fortifications began during a posting to the School of Infantry at Hythe in Kent where he developed an interest in the Martello towers. Later he was posted to Gibraltar, and in 1969 he attended the Australian Army Staff College at Fort Queenscliff, a Victorian coast defence fort near Melbourne. He is a Fellow of the Royal Historical Society, is currently the Chairman of the Fortress Study Group, and his particular interest is in the preservation of fortifications. His published works include *Towers of Strength – Martello Towers Worldwide*; a revised edition of the same book entitled *Martello Towers Worldwide*; and *Defending the North: the Fortifications of Ulster 1798-1956*.

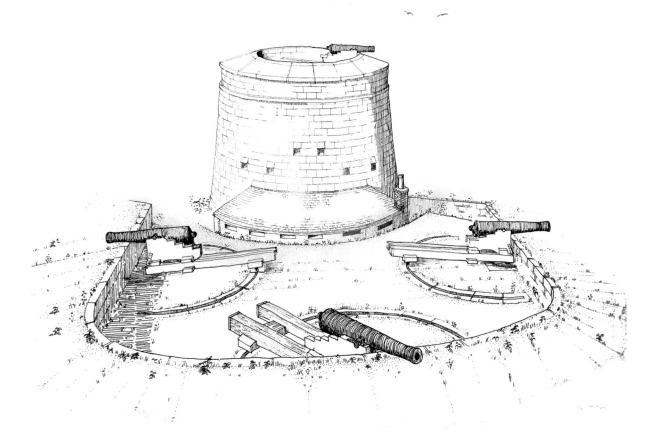

Tower No.7 at Killiney south of Dublin drawn by the late Paul Kerrigan.

AUTHOR'S FOREWORD

In my two earlier books on the Martello towers, *Towers of Strength* and *Martello Towers Worldwide*, I described the origin of the British Martello towers and briefly described the fifty towers built in Ireland, more than were built in any other country except England, the design of many of which was specific to Ireland. However, both books could only describe the Irish towers and their history in a very general manner. So the aim of this book is to detail the history of the Irish towers and describe not only the Martello towers but also the 'quadrangular towers' or defensible guardhouses and also the signal towers built along the Irish coast during the Napoleonic period.

My research has revealed much of the history of these fascinating structures together with details of the characters of the officers of the Royal Engineers who built them. Major General Fisher, Lieutenant Colonels Fenwick and Sir Charles Holloway together with Captain Birch and Captain Sir William Smith are among those who bring life to the story of these towers.

Today most of the towers are still standing, monuments to a dramatic period in Irish history but many are now in poor condition, in a state of dereliction and gradually falling into total ruin. It can only be hoped that their historical importance will be recognised before it is too late and steps can be taken at least to stabilise them and, hopefully, eventually to restore them.

I have enjoyed travelling around Ireland to look at the towers and there are a number of people to whom I am grateful for their help in providing information about the towers and photographs. In particular I am grateful to the late Paul Kerrigan whose own study of the Irish Martello towers pre-dated my own work and who, most kindly, gave me permission to use some of his splendid drawings. I am grateful also to Niall O'Donoghue for providing a photograph of Tower 7 at Loughlinstown which he has so faithfully restored and to Dermot Rainey of Sherry Fitzgerald Rainey for providing aerial photographs of Knockalla Fort on Lough Swilly. I am also particularly grateful to Margaret Pinsent for so kindly proof reading the manuscript for me, and to Martin Brown for drawing the maps.

As always in research of this kind there are a number of organisations and institutions without whose help so willingly given this book could not have been written. My thanks go to the staff of the National Archives at Kew in London; to the Keeper of the Manuscripts and his staff at Trinity College Library in Dublin; to Commandant Kennedy and the staff of the Military Archives in Dublin; and the staff of the Heritage Department of the Department of the Environment in Northern Ireland who opened up the tower at Magilligan Point for me.

Every effort has been made to find the copyright holder of each of the pictures and plans used to illustrate this book and to obtain the appropriate permission to publish. However, if I have unwittingly infringed an owner's copyright I can but apologise and say that I have tried to find the owner but failed!

I hope this book will be of interest to a wide range of readers despite its specialised subject and I also hope, in particular, that it will stir an interest in these fascinating structures that may help to preserve those that currently remain, derelict, abandoned and forlorn.

BILL CLEMENTS

INTRODUCTION

The Irish Defences

In the seventeenth and eighteenth centuries the major seaports of Ireland were defended by a number of fortifications many dating from Cromwell's Protectorate and earlier and mostly in poor condition. Only Duncannon Fort defending the approach to Waterford and Charles Fort defending Kinsale could be considered to be major fortifications and in the eighteenth century the main defence of Ireland was considered to be the Royal Navy. Ports such as Galway, Waterford, Limerick, Londonderry and Carrickfergus relied upon their old town walls and medieval fortifications to defend them from the possibility of an enemy raid. Indeed, the only Irish town to be seriously threatened by an enemy force in the eighteenth century was Carrickfergus which was captured briefly by a small French force under the naval captain Thurot in 1760.

In Cork harbour a small fort, Cove Fort, was built in 1743 but it was not until the American War of Independence that a number of temporary batteries were established to defend Cork and Passage East. In 1783 a large battery for twenty one guns, named Fort Westmoreland in 1790, was constructed on Spike Island and, other than this battery, the only permanent fortifications to be commenced for the defence of Cork were Forts Camden and Carlisle, built to defend the entrance to Cork harbour. Indeed, prior to the outbreak of the Revolutionary War with France in 1793 little attempt was made to improve the Irish defences. However, in 1804 work on a large fortress commenced on Spike Island which replaced the original Fort Westmoreland, which can be seen today. Work on the second Fort Westmoreland proceeded slowly throughout the war with Napoleon and it was not completed until the middle of the nineteenth century.

At the start of the war with France in 1793 a small redoubt, Packenham Redoubt, was built on Tarbert Island in the Shannon Estuary to defend the approach to Limerick but it was the attempted invasions of Ireland by the French in 1796 and 1798 and the failed Irish rebellion in the latter year that forced the British government to concentrate their attention on the permanent defences of Ireland including the construction of the Pigeon House Fort to defend Dublin.

The French Invade

In December 1796 a French invasion force carrying Wolfe Tone, the leader of the United Irishmen, and 15,000 men aboard a fleet of 45 ships, including 17 ships-of-the-line, arrived in Bantry Bay and was only prevented from landing by adverse weather conditions. The French fleet had managed to escape from Brest despite the Royal Navy blockade, though the ship carrying Admiral Morard de Galles and the army commander General Lazare Hoche on leaving Brest became separated from the other ships and, failing to rejoin the fleet, returned to Brest. Of the remaining ships only 15 managed to reach Bantry Bay and this force lay off Bere Island for two days before being forced to weigh anchor when the weather deteriorated and a strong gale blew from the east. When the gale eventually moderated the French were forced to return to Brest from lack of provisions.

The 1798 Rebellion in Ireland encouraged the French Directorate to consider sending another invasion force to Ireland to assist the rebels and so a small force of 4,000 men under the command of General Humbert was despatched in three separate expeditions. Through a lack of co-ordination on the part of the French authorities only General Humbert and 1,200 men aboard three frigates managed to land in Ireland at Killala Bay in County Mayo when the rebellion had been crushed by government forces.

Figure 0.1: The Torre Fiumicelli o Mozza near Otranto in Southern Italy. This tower was constructed in 1582 to guard against Moorish raiders. Note the remains of the *machicoulis* on the parapet. (*Author's photograph*).

After a number of initial successes against yeomanry and militia, and the failure of General Hardy with the bulk of the troops of the invasion force to arrive Humbert surrendered to General Lord Cornwallis at Ballinamuck in September 1798. This second invasion attempt, only two years after the attempt to land in Bantry Bay, when a force of 1,200 men was only defeated after considerable effort on the part of the British forces in Ireland, only served to emphasise Ireland's vulnerability. These events resulted in the construction of a large number of temporary batteries to defend Cork, Bantry Bay and Lough Swilly.

However, it was the outbreak of war once again in 1803 after the collapse of the Treaty of Amiens that saw immediate efforts to improve the defences of the island. With a French army massed on the coast opposite Dover for an imminent invasion it was clear that Ireland was also vulnerable, particularly if the French decided to make a diversionary attack in

conjunction with a landing on the south coast of England. Local commanders were ordered to prepare defences to prevent a French landing and among the works proposed by the officers of the Royal Engineers were gun towers and defensible guardhouses.

The design of the British Martello tower was by no means original. Gun towers had been a feature of the Mediterranean coasts of Spain and Italy for over three hundred years. These simple gun towers had proved to be an effective and economic form of coastal defence protecting small harbours against raids by Barbary pirates and ships of other European powers. Indeed, during the Revolutionary War with France at the end of the 18th century, a tower at Mortella Bay in north west Corsica had successfully held off an attack by two Royal Navy ships, HMS *Fortitude* (74 guns) and HMS *Juno* (32 guns). In 1794 having captured and then abandoned the tower the British returned three months later only to be

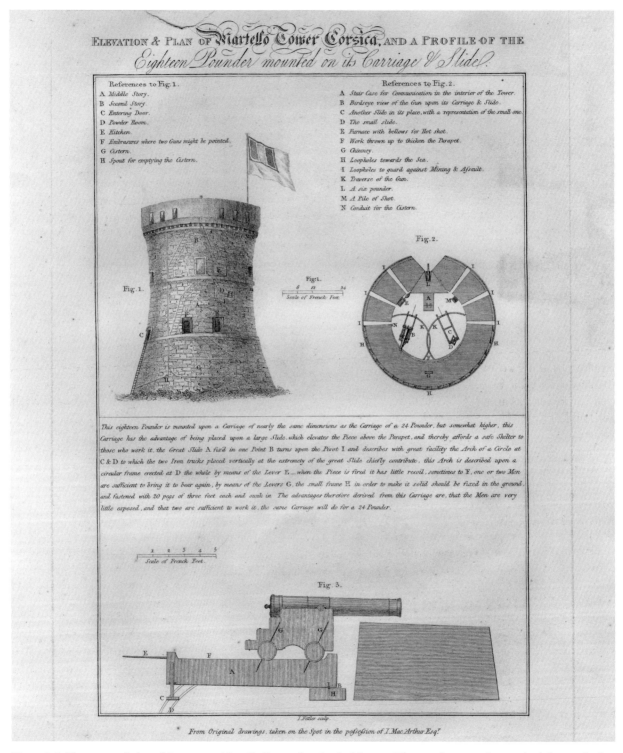

Figure 0.2: Elevation and plan of the tower at Mortella Bay on the island of Corsica. This was the tower that repulsed the attack of two Royal Navy ships in 1796. (*Author's collection*).

Figure 0.3: The tower at Mortella Bay after reconstruction by the Royal Engineers in 1795. (*Author's collection*).

repulsed by the garrison. The two ships bombarded the tower for over two hours and, despite the fact that the tower was armed only with two 18-pounder guns and one small 6-pounder gun, both ships were driven off with considerable loss of men and damage to the ships. It was only after troops were landed and field artillery used to bombard the tower from the rear that it was eventually captured. The British then repaired the tower and occupied it for the next two years, finally withdrawing and destroying the tower with explosives.

The reputation of the tower at Mortella Bay convinced a number of influential officers of the Royal Engineers that the design of the tower presented an effective and economic form of defence for a beach or headland and in 1798 two towers were built in Cape Colony, after its capture from the Dutch, and another on the island of Trinidad. However, it was on the island of Minorca in the Mediterranean, where two towers had been built by the Spanish, that 'Mortella' towers were built in any number. The British reoccupied the island in 1798 and in the next four years the British built a total of eleven towers. Among the officers of the Royal Engineers with the occupying force were a number

who had previously served with the British force in Corsica and in designing the new towers they adopted and adapted the design of both the Corsican and the Spanish towers. At that time these towers were generally referred to as 'Mortella Towers' but the word 'Mortella' seems to have become quite quickly corrupted to 'Martello' and it is by the name 'Martello Towers' that we know them today.

The Minorcan Towers

A total of eleven towers were built by the British on Minorca between 1798 and 1802 closely resembling the Spanish towers. They were circular in shape, and were of two types, large and small. The large towers had a batter to the wall giving them the resemblance of an up-turned flower pot and usually mounted one or two heavy guns. The towers were built of stone with an outer wall with a thickness of up to 13ft (4m) and the entrance was usually at first floor level or through the parapet by means of a ladder that could be withdrawn into the tower. There was a *machicoulis* over the door and inside the tower there were usually two internal chambers with a magazine and store on the ground floor and living accommodation on the first floor. The gun was mounted on top of the tower

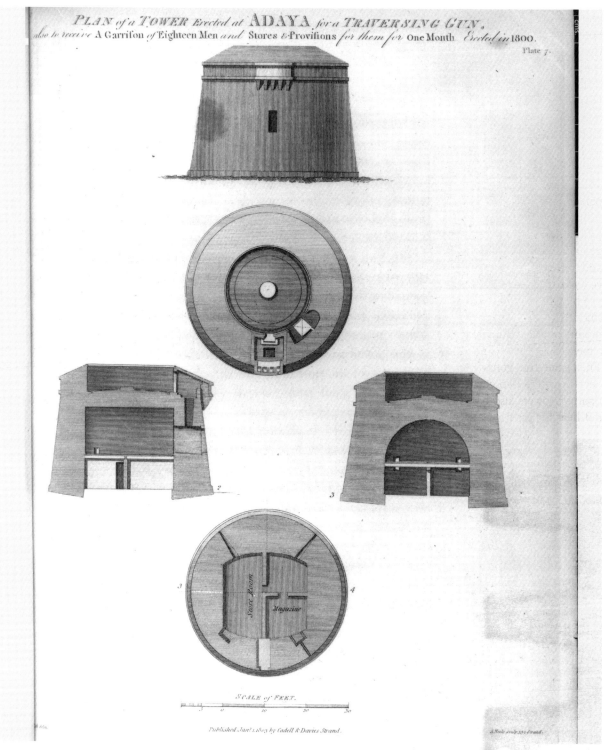

Figure 0.4: Plan & section of the tower built at Addaya on Minorca in 1798. This tower appears to have been the model for the towers built on the coast north and south of Dublin. *(The British Library Board: 583.i.4 opp16)*

and the gun platform was usually supported by a bomb-proof arch. The supply of powder and shot to the gun (or guns) was by means of a passageway in the wall leading to the *machicoulis*.

The towers were of two types, a large tower 36ft (11m) high and 55ft (17m) in diameter and a smaller one 30ft (9.2m) high and 35ft (10.75m) in diameter. General Pasley, who was a Royal Engineers subaltern in Minorca in 1798, describes these towers in his book *A Course of Elementary Fortification* published in 1822. One of the smaller towers, at Santandria, was particularly interesting being smaller than all the others, only 26ft (8m) high. However, it was protected by a ditch and glacis and the ditch was defended with a *caponier* and a counterscarp gallery and this was a design that was to be repeated some years later in Ireland.

The towers mounted one or two heavy 24-pounder smooth-bore guns on the top gun platform, each mounted on a timber traversing platform running on a metal track, or racer, around the base of the parapet. This gave the gun a 360 degree traverse, or 180 degrees where two guns were mounted. Some of the Spanish towers also had furnaces to heat the shot to red-heat for use against ships.

The Board of Ordnance

After the Irish Acts of Union in 1800 the body responsible for the construction of permanent fortifications in Great Britain, Ireland and the Empire and also for the development, production and supply of artillery and other weapons to the army and the Royal Navy was the Board of Ordnance. The Board comprised a mixture of military and civilian officers of whom the senior member was the Master General of the Ordnance who was a member of the Cabinet and the Privy Council and, as such, the government's senior military adviser. Under the Master General came the Lieutenant General of the Ordnance and the Inspector General of Fortifications, the latter being the senior engineer officer of the armed forces and commander of the army's professional corps; the Royal Artillery, the Royal Engineers which was an all-officer corps, and, from its formation in 1813, the corps of Royal Sappers and Miners.

The four principal civilian officers were the Surveyor General, the Storekeeper General, the Clerk of the Deliveries and the Clerk of the Ordnance. Subordinate to these officers were two principal permanent civil servants, the Secretary to the Ordnance and the Chief Clerk to the Clerk of

Figure 0.5: The Santandria tower on Minorca. Sited low within a surrounding *glacis* this tower would appear to be the model for the Cathcart Tower on Bere Island. (*Author's photograph*).

the Ordnance. The Master General and the Inspector General of Fortifications assisted by the two civil servants formed a small executive committee responsible for the day-to-day decisions made in the name of the Board of Ordnance. When the Board and the Inspector General required advice on the construction, modification or repair of permanent fortifications it would be advised by a body known as a Committee of Engineers, comprising two or more senior officers of the Royal Engineers. In each military district there was a Commanding Royal Engineer with a number of officers subordinate to him. In Ireland the Commanding Royal Engineer had his headquarters in Dublin but when the decision was taken to fortify Cork Harbour a Commanding Royal Engineer was appointed for the Cork District who reported directly to the Inspector General of Fortifications in London. The Commanding Royal Engineer, together with the senior Royal Artillery officer, was a member of a body known as the Respective Officers. This body was a miniature reflection of the Board of Ordnance itself and included the Surveyor, Storekeeper and Clerk appointed, in Ireland, to the Dublin military district and these officers supervised expenditure in all the Irish military districts.

Prior to the Acts of Union there had existed in Ireland a separate Ordnance establishment and Corps of Royal Engineers in Ireland comprising eight officers under the command of Major General Charles Vallencey. This body was disbanded in 1801 with only one officer, First Lieutenant George Armit, transferring to the Corps of Royal Engineers. From 1802 to 1811 the Commanding Royal Engineer in Dublin was Lieutenant Colonel, later Brigadier General, Benjamin Fisher, an interesting and talented engineer and artist. Sadly he suffered from fits of depression, probably as a result of earlier service in the West Indies, and, possibly because of this, while in Dublin he had a long-running feud with the other Respective Officers. The feud only ended when he was posted to Portsmouth on promotion to major general where, in 1814, he died by his own hand.

Among the other engineer officers in Ireland serving under Fisher there were a number that had served previously in Minorca and there can be little

doubt that the strong resemblance between the early Irish Martello towers and those built by the British on Minorca resulted from the previous experience of those officers on that island. These officers included Captain Birch who worked in Bantry Bay and who advised Lord Cathcart, the Commander-in-Chief in Ireland, on the construction of the Dublin Bay towers. Other officers with experience of Minorca were Captain Cardew who was in charge of the construction of the later fortifications on the shores of Lough Swilly, and Lieutenant George Dyson, who died in Jamaica in 1806.

The Twiss Report

In 1798 the new Commander-in-Chief in Ireland, General Sir Ralph Abercromby, produced, during his short tenure in command, a memorandum on the defence of Ireland for the Lord Lieutenant. In it he emphasised the importance of protecting Cork and Limerick together with Bantry Bay, the Shannon Estuary and Lough Swilly. The Rebellion of 1798 acted as a spur to the construction of coastal defences, the majority of which were 'Field Works', temporary defences built on the authority of a commander-in-chief and financed by the Treasury rather than by the Board of Ordnance in Ireland which, as we have seen, was responsible for the construction of permanent fortifications.

General Abercromby's memorandum was followed by a report by Colonel Alexander Hope, the Adjutant General, in 1801 which, in turn, was commented on by Lieutenant General Dundas, the Quartermaster General, and these were passed by the Duke of York to the Master General of the Ordnance, Lieutenant General the Earl of Chatham. The result was that Colonel William Twiss, the Commanding Royal Engineer of the Southern District in England, was despatched to Ireland on 26th July 1802 to make a report for the Master General on how that country could best be defended.

Twiss reported on 15th January 1803 and laid down the priorities for defence as being; the security of Dublin; the establishment of supply depots with good communications by water with England; the security of the harbours of Cork, Waterford and Limerick; and the defence of the important anchorages of Bantry

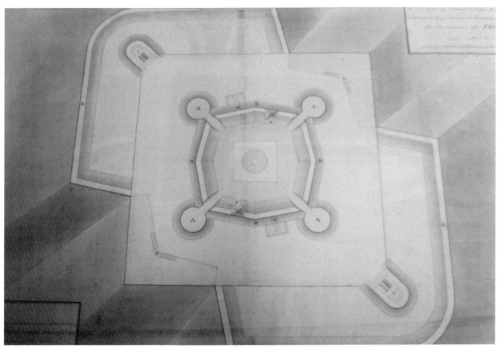

Figure 0.6: Plan for a large casemated tower designed by Colonel Twiss RE. This plan accompanied his 1803 report on the defence of Ireland. (*TNA WO 55/831*).

Bay and Lough Swilly. Colonel Twiss was particularly anxious to ensure that his recommendations should be practicable and avoid unnecessary expense. The section of the report dealing with Bantry Bay showed Twiss at his most percipient. Referring to Berehaven, or Bear Island as he called it, he said: 'This harbour has two entrances both of which might be rendered difficult by Fortification, but could scarcely ever be made impassable and the extent of the Island is such, that no fortress could secure the possession of it, without a numerous Garrison'.[1] In Colonel Twiss's view any enemy entering Bantry Bay would land troops at the head of the bay in Glengarriff Harbour or from the anchorage between Whiddy Island and Bantry Town, so the answer was to strengthen the defences of these locations with permanent fortifications. He proposed the construction of large casemated towers similar to the ones he had already recommended for the defence of Enniskillen, though these towers were really substantial redoubts rather than the Martello towers which came later.

It is, perhaps, interesting to note that in the following year Colonel Twiss, now having been promoted to brigadier general, suggested the construction of two similar large towers for the

defence of the Kent and Sussex coasts. However, these towers when built were not the elaborate towers proposed in his original Irish report but were actually circular redoubts. They were built in 1805-06 at Dymchurch, near Folkestone in Kent, and at Eastbourne in Sussex.

The Martello Towers

The first Martello towers to be constructed in the British Isles were built in Ireland to defend the anchorage of Berehaven between Bere Island and Castletownbere in Bantry Bay. These towers were constructed as a result of a request from Rear Admiral Sir Robert Calder who commanded a Royal Navy squadron based in Bantry Bay and who was anxious about the protection of his supply ships anchored in Berehaven. The Bere Island towers were followed by twenty six towers to defend Dublin and built at the instigation of the Lord Lieutenant.

In England seventy four towers and two circular redoubts were built along the coast of Kent and Sussex at Brigadier General Twiss's suggestion. Subsequently, between 1808 and 1811 a further twenty nine towers and a circular redoubt were built along the coast of Essex and Suffolk. Unlike the Irish towers those built to defend the English coast were of two standard types. The South Coast towers were elliptical in shape averaging approximately 30ft (9.2m) in height and were built of brick rather than stone. Each South Coast tower was designed to mount a single heavy gun while the East Coast towers were cam-shaped in plan, of a similar height but a larger diameter, and were also built of brick. They mounted a heavier armament of one heavy gun and two smaller guns, either howitzers or carronades. These towers were built initially as a major defence against the possible invasion of England by Napoleon's Grand Army ranged along the French coast from Holland to Le Havre.

In Ireland Martello towers were seen as a cheap and effective coast fortification and some fifty two towers

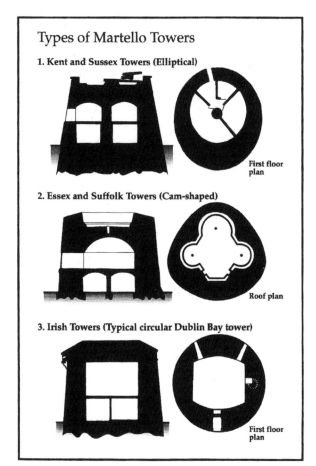

Figure 0.7: Types of English and Irish Martello Towers. (*Michael Pugh*).

were built in two phases, the first phase between 1804 and 1806 and the second between 1810 and 1815. In the first phase, in addition to the four towers on Bere Island, twenty six towers were built to defend Dublin, twelve to the north of the city and fourteen to the south. In the same period a tower was built on Garinish Island in Glengarriff Harbour near the town of Bantry and two further towers in Wexford and Waterford, one to defend Rosslare Harbour and the other on Baginbun Point near Fethard-on-Sea. In addition, three circular batteries were built on Whiddy Island to defend Bantry. These early Irish towers generally resembled the British towers built on the island of Minorca but there was also a number of larger towers mounting two heavy guns and using a gun mounting that was unique to Ireland.

In the second phase, resulting from a continuing threat of invasion and a new threat of war with the United States, a further eighteen towers were built; five for the defence of Cork harbour; three for the protection of Galway; six on the shores of Lough Swilly and Lough Foyle in Counties Donegal and Londonderry; two to defend the rear of Duncannon Fort in County Wexford; and two were built on the upper reaches of the Shannon to defend crossings at Banagher and Meelick. Unlike the towers built in the first phase most of these later towers were built to designs closely resembling either the English South or East Coast designs.

The Irish Martello towers built in the first building phase were constructed as what were termed 'Field Works', which meant that their construction was ordered by the Commander-in-Chief in Dublin and funded by money provided directly from the Treasury rather than authorised and financed by the Board of Ordnance. This ensured a speedy construction programme suitable for emergency situations such as a threat of invasion and so circumvented the usual delays involved when the Board was involved in authorising such construction. 'Field Works' were usually exactly what the term implied, turf and sod defences built hurriedly to meet an emergency situation. However, many of the Irish defences built as 'Field Works', including the Martello towers, were actually constructed of stone and resembled in every way the permanent defences more usually authorised by the Board of Ordnance. This resulted in a conflict with the Board of Ordnance when the Board was asked to take over the payment of the maintenance of these fortifications in 1806. The Board of Ordnance was most reluctant to take responsibility for the upkeep of the Irish towers, surmising, correctly, that it would incur considerable expense in their maintenance. Negotiations were protracted and it was not until 1811 that the Board finally accepted responsibility for all the towers and their adjacent batteries.

Throughout their history the manning of the towers was always a problem. Unlike the situation in England where there were Volunteer artillery corps there were very few such corps in Ireland, though one, the Loyal Loughlinstown Yeomanry Gunners, manned batteries at Athlone and on the shores of the Shannon estuary. Soldiers from the Veteran and Garrison battalions manned the Bere Island and Dublin towers, while the Lough Swilly towers were left in the hands of a local Yeomanry regiment, the Rathmullen Yeomanry, the men of which were taught the 'Great gun exercise' as, indeed, were some regular regiments in England, including the Connaught Rangers, as late as the 1890s.

After 1815 and the end of the war with Napoleon the garrisons were reduced, usually to one or two Royal Artillery gunners and a number of NCOs and private soldiers of a line regiment. The latter acted as guards to prevent the local population stealing the stone and timber from the towers. In 1823 only at Bere Island, at Tarbert on the Shannon and Buncrana on the shores of Lough Swilly was there an officer in charge. However, by the middle of the century many towers were unoccupied, the responsibility of a Master Gunner or non-commissioned officer stationed in one of the nearby forts, while others were in the charge of a pensioner and occupied by his family. By the end of the century virtually all had been abandoned and either rented out, sold, or the land returned to the original owner.

Although the Irish Martello towers were constructed primarily to defend the island against a French invasion during the war against Napoleon the towers remained an integral part of Ireland's defences until well after the Crimean War. A number were up-gunned with heavier guns mounted on their gun platforms, some were used by the Coastguard while a number of towers were used in each of the World Wars. One tower, on Bere Island in Bantry Bay, was used as the Port War Signal Station for Berehaven anchorage in the First World War while in the Second World War the Magilligan tower in County Londonderry was used as the Battery Observation Post for an emergency coast defence battery and two of the Dublin towers appear to have been used by the Coastwatching Service during the 'Emergency'. Today the majority of the towers still stand, many converted to private residences and one or two are now open to the public as museums or ancient monuments.

This is the story of all the Irish Martello towers and quadrangular towers, also known as defensible guardhouses and unique to Ireland, and signal towers built during the nineteenth century and as such it is a record of an important part of the island's military heritage.

Chapter 1

THE BANTRY TOWERS

The Garinish Island Tower

The abortive French invasion of Ireland in 1796 had been aimed at Bantry Bay and this was followed two years later by the landing of a small French force in Killalla Bay in County Mayo all of which served to reinforce the British government's view that Ireland was Britain's Achilles Heel. Initial efforts to fortify Bantry Bay after the attempted landing in 1796 resulted in the construction of a number of small batteries each of one and two guns and built of sod and earth which were sited to defend the town of Bantry. In addition, and resulting from Colonel Twiss's report of 1803, the Board of Ordnance gave authority for three circular redoubts, one armed with twelve guns and the other two with eight guns each, to be built on Whiddy Island and a single-gun tower and a small battery on Garinish Island in Glengariff Harbour, to the north west of Bantry Town.

The Garinish tower was a rather small tower built of rubble stone standing only 25ft (7.6m) high and had a base diameter of 37ft (11.3m) and a wall thickness of 8ft (2.45 m). There was only a slight batter to the wall and there was no bomb-proof roof supporting the gun platform which originally mounted a 32-pounder carronade which, by 1809, had been changed to a single, obsolescent, 8-in (203-mm) brass howitzer. The doorway was at first-floor level but was only about 7ft 6 inches (2.3m) above the ground and the door itself was placed at the chamber end on the inner rather than the outer side of the wall thus providing a short corridor. This was a weak point in the design of the tower since an attacking force could place an explosive charge in the corridor to blow open the door as Captain Lord Cochrane RN had done to a Spanish tower in the Mediterranean. The tower was completed in August 1806 and in 1808 a report noted that: 'The tower is designed for 16 men in four double bedsteads. The wall of the tower is coped with brick and to make it more secure is covered with slates.'[1]

The adjoining battery of three guns was constructed in front of the tower and was U-shaped with the *terreplein* and parapet built onto a rocky outcrop and with high masonry walls on either flank. On one side there was a passage from the entrance in the rear wall of the battery with steps providing access to the *banquette* running along the side walls and the *terreplein*. Adjoining the entrance passage were two chambers, one used as a guardroom and the other providing accommodation for the officer-in-charge. The guns of the battery, mounted as they were on the highest point of the island, covered the immediate anchorage effectively and the howitzer on the tower provided a defence against an infantry assault. However, the guns of the battery were too distant from Whiddy Island to be able to provide any support for the redoubts there.

The first tower on Garinish Island was complete by the end of 1805 but in 1809 Brigadier General Trotter RA reported that the magazine in the tower was too small to enable powder barrels to be opened and cartridges filled within the magazine. He requested that a barrack for one NCO and 12 gunners be erected on the island together with a small laboratory where the cartridges could be filled and a storeroom for the Gunner. This request was approved and the

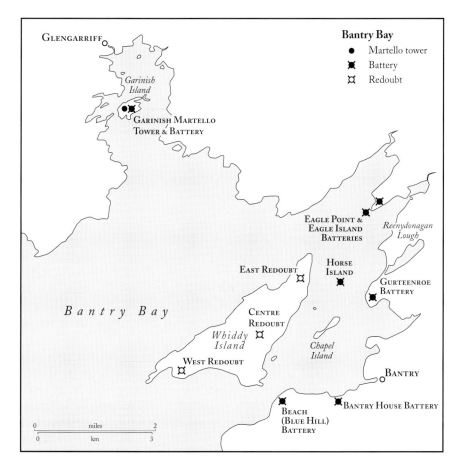

Figure 1.1: The towers, redoubts and batteries of Bantry Bay. (*Martin Brown*)

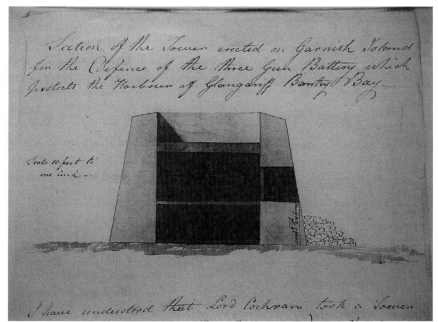

Figure 1.2: A sketch of the Garinish Island tower as originally constructed which shows the poor design of the door and entrance passage which was vulnerable to an enemy attack. (*TNA WO 55/832*).

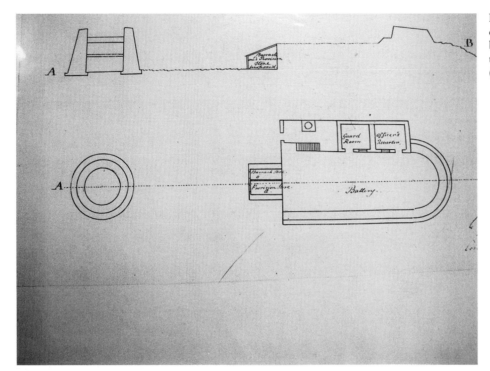

Figure 1.3: Plan of the original Garinish Island battery & tower 1808, prior to its later rebuilding. *(TNA WO 55/832).*

barrack erected in the rear of the battery.[2] However, as early as 1808 the tower was in poor condition and although the guns were still mounted in the battery the post was not occupied by troops and by 1812 parts of the tower had collapsed. Lieutenant Colonel Fenwick, the Commanding Royal Engineer in Cork, decided to take this opportunity to replace the old tower with a large tower to be built to the same design as that to be used in the construction of five towers proposed for the defence of Cork Harbour. However, in April 1813 the Inspector General of Fortifications, Lieutenant General Mann, rejected

Figure 1.4: An old postcard showing the Garinish Island battery & tower as they were in the late 19th century. *(Author's collection).*

Figure 1.5: The Garinish Island tower today. The photograph shows the tower as it was reconstructed by Lieutenant Colonel Fenwick RE in 1812. (*Author's photograph*).

Fisher's plan. In a letter dated 4th April 1813 Fenwick was informed that the Inspector General 'does not concur with you in the expediency of rebuilding the Tower in a larger construction'[3] and would not approve the expense involved in the construction of a large tower. So Fisher rebuilt the tower to a similar design to the Cork towers but on a reduced scale.

The Garinish tower was rebuilt in rubble stone rather than the limestone ashlar used in the Cork towers, a further saving in the cost of construction, and, like the Cork towers, it was drum-shaped without a batter to the wall as Fisher believed a vertical wall reduced rain damage to the tower, an important consideration in Ireland! When rebuilt the tower was included as an integral part of the battery and the battery walls were flush with the wall of the tower close to each of the two windows on either side of the door, giving the whole a roughly triangular shape.

There was also a bomb-proof arch enabling the solid stone roof to support a heavy gun, possibly a 12-pounder, using an unserviceable cannon as a pivot. The entrance was still at first floor level but the door was now flush with the exterior wall of the tower rather than at the end of a short passage as in the earlier tower. In the first-floor living quarters there was a single fireplace and there no longer appears to have been separate accommodation for an officer.

In 1835 the Master General of the Ordnance ordered that all batteries in Ireland not required for the protection of merchant shipping should be dismantled[4]. Although it was decided that not all the Martello towers should be given up it is likely that the Garinish tower and battery had already been abandoned at this time for in 1827 the island had been leased to Lord Bantry and in 1861 a report on the Irish defences by Lieutenant Colonel Westmacott RA stated that the small work on Garinish Island had 'been allowed to fall into ruins'.[5]

Today the Garinish tower stands refurbished in the famous Ilnacullin garden on the island, an Italianate garden designed by Harold Peto in the early years of the twentieth century for the Belfast-born businessman Annan Bryce. The battery, however, is derelict with only two walls standing but the tower is in good condition and an integral part of the garden design.

The Whiddy Island 'Towers'

In June 1803 Lieutenant Colonel Sir Charles Holloway, the Commanding Royal Engineer of the Cork District, travelled to Bantry and reported his findings concerning the fortification of Bantry, to the Inspector General of Fortifications in London. On concluding his inspection Sir Charles submitted his own plan for a redoubt to be built on Whiddy Island. This was a simpler design for a circular redoubt sited within a deep ditch but it retained Twiss's concept of a circular tower armed with a single gun in the centre and this plan was accepted by the Inspector General of Fortifications.

Construction of the Whiddy Island fortifications was authorised on 15th July 1803 and supervision of the work was initially delegated by Lieutenant Colonel Holloway to Lieutenant Birch, a talented Royal Engineers officer who had recently been posted to Ireland from Minorca where he had been involved in the construction of some of the first Martello towers. The initial plan was for the construction of only two 'towers' or circular redoubts on land owned by Lord Bantry but it soon became clear from on-the-spot inspections that just two redoubts, one at the western end and one at the eastern end of the island, would be insufficient to prevent an enemy landing on the island and taking the redoubts by assault. There would have to be a third redoubt in the centre of the island that would ensure that all three redoubts would be defended by mutually supporting fire.

It is not clear from the existing records when the decision was taken to construct a third redoubt but by March 1804 work was well underway on the three redoubts. The Centre Redoubt was to be the largest of the three, mounting twelve 24-pounder SBML guns and having accommodation for 150 men. The East and West Redoubts were to be smaller, each mounting eight guns and having accommodation for 100 men. It is also clear that by this date the idea of

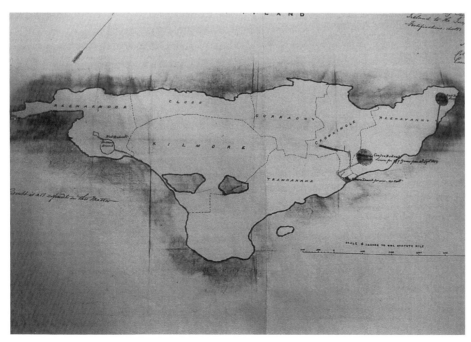

Figure 1.6: Map of Whiddy Island showing the location of the three redoubts. (*TNA WO 44/120*).

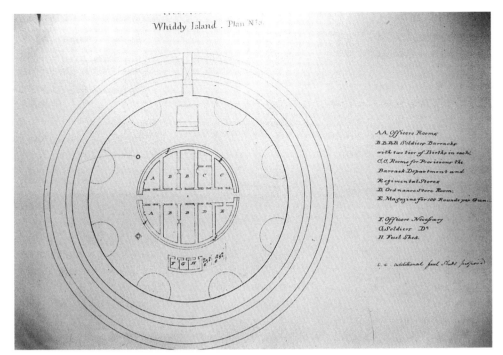

Whiddy Island . Plan Nᵒ 3.

AA. *Officers Rooms*
B.B.BB *Soldiers Barracks*
with two tier of Births in each.
C.C. *Rooms for Provisions the*
Barrack Department and
Regimental Stores
D *Ordnance Store Room.*
E. *Magazine for 100 Rounds pr Gun.*

F. *Officers Necessary*
G.Soldiers *Dᵒ*
H. *Fuel Shed.*

c. c *additional fuel Sheds proposed*

Figure 1.7: Plan of the West Redoubt on Whiddy Island. This redoubt, together with the other two redoubts on the island resembled the redoubts built at the same time in England at Dymchurch, Eastbourne and Harwich. (*TNA WO 55/832*).

a central tower in each redoubt had been dropped.

All three redoubts were surrounded by a ditch and glacis, the glacis formed from the excavated earth from the ditch, and so very little of the redoubt wall was visible above the glacis. Each redoubt had a single entrance approached by means of a drawbridge across the ditch which in the Centre Redoubt was to be 34ft (10.46m) deep and that of the West Redoubt 18ft (5.5m) deep. Rock prevented the full excavation of the East Redoubt ditch where the contractor was unable to reach the required depth of 18ft (5.5 m).

The Centre Redoubt had a diameter of 250ft (77m) and the East and West Redoubts were smaller, each with a diameter of 210ft (64.6m). With the dropping of the plan to build a central tower in each redoubt bomb-proof barrack buildings were substituted for the towers. These buildings provided accommodation, storerooms and magazines and were vaulted with brick to provide protection from high-angle fire from mortars and howitzers. In the Centre and East Redoubts each had three ranges of buildings sited parallel to each other in the centre of each redoubt. In the West Redoubt, however, there were two large semi-circular structures with a passage between them. It would appear from the records that

the alteration in the design of the bomb-proof buildings in the West Redoubt originated with the Board of Ordnance in London. In October 1804 the Inspector General of Fortifications wrote to Sir Charles Holloway instructing him to change the design of the buildings in all three redoubts. Holloway replied that in the Centre and East redoubts construction of the buildings was so far advanced that it would be extremely costly to initiate changes at this stage of the contract. However, in the West Redoubt work on the buildings had not begun so it was possible to build them to the new design.

The armament of the redoubts comprised 24-pounder SBML guns on traversing platforms. These were sited around the circular edge of each redoubt firing *en barbette* over a parapet varying between 12 and 14ft (3.6 and 4.3m) in thickness. The traversing platforms were mounted on front pivots and along the inner base of the parapet there was a *banquette* for infantrymen to fire from.

Construction of these three redoubts was a major operation and at the height of the building work the contractor, a Mr Thomas Mahoney, employed more than 1,000 men on the construction sites. In March 1805 it was recorded that 618 men and 60 horses were employed on the Centre Redoubt, 214 men and 15 horses at the West Redoubt and 174 men and 12 horses at the East Redoubt. The final cost to the Board of Ordnance of the three redoubts was £24,917 0s.11p compared to the contractor's original estimate of £22,209 17s. 0d. The Centre Redoubt was finally completed in September 1806, the East Redoubt in September 1807 and the West Redoubt two months later. However, in 1808 the forts were not considered in a state of defence through lack of storage for provisions.[6]

After the end of the war with Napoleon in 1815 the Whiddy Island redoubts were maintained in the charge of a Master Gunner and four gunners with a small infantry detachment, all these being withdrawn in 1829 and replaced by a pensioner as caretaker. In 1835 the Master General of the Ordnance ordered that all batteries in Ireland not required for the protection of merchant shipping should be dismantled and two years later, in 1837, the Board of Ordnance ordered that all the ordnance under charge at Whiddy Island should be returned to Woolwich. By 1861 the Whiddy Island redoubts were the only works in Bantry Bay still in comparatively substantial repair and they can still be seen today, heavily overgrown and access is only possible to the Centre Redoubt.

The Bere Island Towers

Bere Island (also sometimes called Beer or Bear Island) is situated close to the northern shore of Bantry Bay and near the entrance to the bay. It provides a secure deepwater anchorage which, if not previously known to the British Admiralty, was certainly drawn to their attention in 1796 after the arrival of a French fleet in the bay. The island has an area of just under 5,000 acres (1,825 hectares) and in 1803 was bleak, desolate and had a population of just over 1,500 people. The main centre of population was at Lawrence Cove, a sheltered inlet on the north eastern side of the island. There were no roads on the island and only a footpath linking Lawrence Cove with the west of the island.

Earlier in 1803 Lord Hardwicke, the Lord Lieutenant, had asked the Admiralty to station a squadron of ships in Bantry Bay and in December 1803 he wrote to the Rt Hon Charles Yorke, Secretary of State for the Home Department, saying: 'I cannot conclude without expressing, in the strongest manner, my acknowledgements of the attention of His Majesty's Ministers to the Naval defence of Ireland, by the stationing of a Fleet in Bantry Bay.[7]

The squadron was under the command of Rear Admiral Sir Robert Calder who, shortly after arriving in Bantry Bay in his flagship HMS *Prince of Wales* (98 guns), wrote to the Chief Secretary, the Rt Hon William Wickham, asking that fortifications should be built on Bere Island as a matter of urgency, in order to protect the Berehaven anchorage. On 22nd December 1803 he wrote: I have just received official Accounts that I may expect daily to arrive here, nine or ten victuallers and Store Ships with Provisions for Eight Thousand men for four, and Stores for this squadron for six months; it therefore becomes necessary to provide for the protection of these vessels whilst here, particularly so when I am obliged to be at sea with the Squadron. I have examined the Inlet or Creek in the Centre of Berehaven Island, and find it will contain these vessels in perfect safety from all weather, and they will be there ready to supply the Squadron with the greatest dispatch, which is of the utmost importance to the Service I am employed on'.[8]

The Chief Secretary, obviously appreciating the urgency of Rear Admiral Calder's request, wrote with admirable promptitude to the Commander-in-Chief, General Lord Cathcart, recommending that fortifications should be constructed on the island. Continuing on down the chain of command Lord Cathcart wrote to Sir Charles Holloway, the Commanding Royal Engineer for the Cork District, saying: 'My object is to construct some Batteries with Towers or other works to defend them in the most expeditious manner at the Entrance and particularly the Eastern or upper Entrance of Bear (sic) Haven – and that these Works shall be defrayed as Field Works by Government and not upon Ordnance Estimate'.[9] He went on to ask that an officer of the Royal Engineers should be made available to supervise the construction of the batteries and towers.

This request from Lord Cathcart was to place Sir

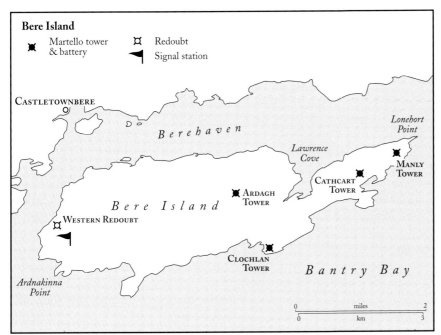

Figure 1.8: Bere Island towers. (*Martin Brown*)

Charles Holloway in a most invidious position and highlights the inherent problem that could arise when permanent fortifications were initiated by a commander-in-chief rather than by the Board of Ordnance. Although field works were normally expected to be temporary defences thrown up quickly to meet an immediate threat the Commander-in-Chief in Ireland envisaged much more permanent defences which would normally be the responsibility of the Board of Ordnance to authorise and fund. Such permanent works needed a trained military engineer to supervise their construction but there was a shortage of Royal Engineers and in 1803 there were only a dozen or so such officers in Ireland all of whom were engaged in Board of Ordnance work. In the last resort Lord Cathcart authorised Sir Charles Holloway to employ a civil engineer if a Royal Engineers officer was not available, but clearly this would not have been as satisfactory as employing a trained military engineer.

It would seem that the Commander-in-Chief had a certain Captain Birch RE in mind since he asked specifically that Captain Birch RE should be detached from Whiddy Island, where he was super-vising the construction of the three redoubts, to inspect Bere Island and prepare a plan for its defence.

Birch had been involved in the construction of the towers on Minorca between 1798 and 1802 when stationed on the island and he recommended the building of towers on Bere Island as early as May 1804.[10] Not all the senior officers in Ireland approved of his proposal and in a letter to Lord Sheffield, dated 20th December 1804, Colonel Henry Clinton, the Quartermaster-General in Ireland, complained, '…the Engineer, Captain Birch, your protegee [sic] who is a great favourite of Lord Cathcart and every Lady I meet, but with whom I cannot agree in his scheme of fortification, he is bit by Martello towers or defensible guard houses'.[11]

The Commander-in-Chief wrote to Sir Charles Holloway asking that Birch 'should be charged with the Direction and execution of these Works without however suspending or interrupting the regular Works in which he is engaged at Whiddy, but for any occasional absence from the latter Place on this Service I must make myself answerable from the urgency of the Service'.[12] This could only be a pious hope since the supervision of the Whiddy Island redoubts and the tower and battery on Garinish Island was more than enough work for the single officer of the Royal Engineers at Bantry.

This placed Sir Charles on the horns of a dilemma

since to meet Lord Cathcart's wishes meant that he was likely to incur the displeasure of the Inspector General of Fortifications in London and vice versa. His answer was to despatch Captain Birch to Bere Island while at the same time reporting his action to the Inspector General. Lieutenant General Morse immediately instructed Sir Charles to order Birch to return to his duty at Whiddy Island and told Sir Charles that he should 'on no account allow any person serving under his command to be drawn from the particular services entrusted to his direction'.[13] Sir Charles Holloway then had the unenviable task of writing to Lord Cathcart to explain the instructions he had received and the commander of the forces answered his letter immediately telling Sir Charles that he must, of course, obey the order he had received from the Inspector General of Fortifications.[14]

The matter soon reached the attention of the Master General of the Ordnance, Lord Chatham. Sir Evan Nepean wrote to Lord Chatham explaining that while Lord Cathcart fully understood that Sir Charles Holloway must obey the order from the Inspector General of Fortifications he asked that Birch might superintend the works occasionally. Lord Chatham's reply is interesting and seems to indicate a politician looking for a compromise acceptable to both parties: 'I found from General Morse that he was so anxious that the principle of not diverting the Officers of the Engineers employed on Stationary Works under the Ordnance, should not be broke in upon, and his apprehension so strong of the evil consequences to the Public Service, likely to result from any such interference, that I felt it quite impossible for me to direct that any direct permission should be sent, for Captain Birch to be employed, even occasionally at Bear [sic] Island, and I besides considered that any such step might be looked upon as a sort of acquiescence on my part, in the present prevailing system of Field Works carrying on, without the authority of the Ordnance'.[15] That having been said he went on to suggest that Lieutenant General Morse should suspend for some weeks repeating his order to Sir Charles Holloway, which would give time for Lord Cathcart's intentions to be fulfilled, or enable him to call on Colonel Fisher, the commanding Royal Engineer in Dublin, for further assistance.

Poor Sir Charles! Caught between a rock and a hard place and he was to run into further trouble some months later when, once again, Lord Cathcart poached Captain Birch to advise him on the construction of Martello towers on the coast immediately to the north and south of Dublin which were also to be constructed as 'Field Works'. This time Holloway incurred the severe displeasure of the Master General of the Ordnance. He just couldn't win and so no doubt he was pleased to see Birch leave Ireland in November 1805 to join his patron Lord Cathcart who had also left Ireland to command the expedition to Hanover. Supervision of the works on the island then became the responsibility of Lieutenant Todd of the Royal Staff Corps, a body formed by, and responsible to, the Quartermaster General in order to supervise the construction of field works and bridges because of the shortage of Royal Engineers officers.

Despite being based in Bantry Captain Birch must have found the journey to Bere Island long and arduous and the reconnaissance even more so. Some years later Lieutenant Colonel Fenwick, who had replaced Sir Charles Holloway as Commanding Royal Engineer at Cork, remembered: 'At the commencement of these works (on Bere Island) there was not a vestige of a Road to the mountains on which most of the Towers and Batteries have been erected, not even a track or footpath but every article of material obliged to be carried on men's shoulders, that most of the materials were obliged to be sent from Cork, that difficulties and impediments were perpetually occurring from the inclemency of the weather on that part of the coast and from the difficulties of getting workmen'.[16]

Birch's plan for the defence of Berehaven involved defending both the eastern and western entrances to the anchorage. The western anchorage was very narrow, only about 350yds (323m) wide between Naglas Point and the nearest point on the mainland, Piper's Point. Here Birch planned to build a redoubt for four 24-pounder SBML guns protected by a round tower while two round towers with associated batteries were planned for the defence of the eastern entrance, one at Lonehort Point and the other at Rerrin. The armament of these towers was two 24-pounder

Figure 1.9: A watercolour of the Cathcart Tower (Tower No.2) on Bere Island painted in 1825 by Lt Alcock RA. This tower differed markedly from the other three towers on Bere Island. (*Courtesy of the National Army Museum, London*).

guns with two 24-pounder SBML guns in a sodwork battery nearby. In addition, the tower at Rerrin was armed with two 13-in (330-mm) mortars mounted in the glacis of the tower. Birch planned a further two towers and two 2-gun batteries, one on the high ground of Ardagh overlooking the hamlet of Lawrence Cove and the other at Clochlan West to secure the shore south of Rerrin. These last two towers were slightly smaller than the Rerrin and Lonehort towers and each mounted a single 24-pounder SBML gun and they and the batteries were sited with a view to defending the land approach to Lawrence Cove. Each 24-pounder gun was provided with 100 rounds of ammunition consisting of 50 round shot, 20 rounds of grapeshot, 10 rounds of case shot and 10 spherical shells. The mortars were each supplied with 30 spherical shells.

The towers were constructed of rubble stone and varied in size with the tower at Clochlan Point on the southern shore being the smallest. All the towers had a batter to the wall and a *machicoulis* over the doorway which was at first-floor level and the

Clochlan tower and the Cathcart Tower were surrounded by dry ditches. Each tower had two floors and a bomb-proof, vaulted roof supporting the gun platform on top. There was no central pillar supporting the gun platform and the living accommodation was divided into three sections with a fireplace in the largest section. The ground floor was used as a magazine. At first-floor level there were two windows and a staircase built into the wall which provided access to the gun platform and the magazine. On the gun platform there was a central pivot and iron racers for the gun or guns that were rear-pivot mounted in Towers Nos. 1 and 2 (also known as Manly and Cathcart Towers) and centre-pivot mounted in Towers Nos. 3 and 4. There was also a furnace for heating shot built into the parapet of the gun platform and on the outer wall of each tower there was a string course level with the floor of the gun platform.

The dimensions of the towers varied but the smallest, Tower No.3, had a height of 26ft (8.1m) and a base diameter of 38ft (11.6m). The Cathcart Tower

Figure 1.10: Plan & section of the Cathcart Tower on Bere Island. *(TNA WO 55/832).*

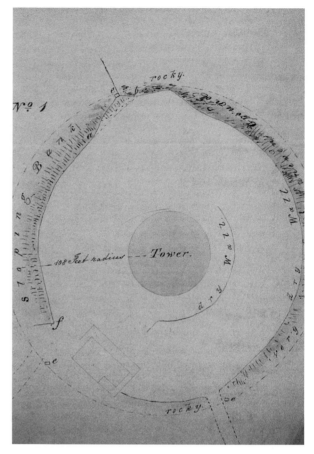

Figure 1.11: Plan of Manly Tower (Tower No.1) on Bere Island. *(TNA WO 55/832).*

(Tower No.2) was somewhat larger with a height of 28ft (8.6m) and a diameter of 41ft (12.6m). This latter tower was a much stronger fortification than any of the other towers, probably because it was the main position defending Lawrence Cove, and showed Birch's Minorca experience through its similarity to the Santandria Tower on that island.

In 1824 Lieutenant Alcock RA visited Bere Island and recorded in his notebook a full description of the Cathcart Tower. Alcock regarded this tower as being 'the most remarkable and best possible defence in the island'. He went on: 'It consists of a common Martello tower twenty eight feet high and one hundred and thirty feet round the base with a dry ditch fourteen feet wide. Under the glacis are case-mated barracks for the troops of the Royal Artillery and a magazine capable of containing two hundred

and eighty barrels of gunpowder. The method of access to the ditch is by a *pas de souris* in the western angle of the sallyport. The access to the top of the tower is by a ladder that reaches to a door cut half way in its height. The windows of the opposite case-mates being so constructed at the same time as to show a cross fire of musquetry [*sic*] on the "sole" of the sallyport in question. The magazine is also very well protected being covered by the Tower on the north and by its own glacis in the south, and as to the case-mated barracks which is calculated to hold forty eight men, it is like most quarters of the kind not the most desirable residence for a soldier'.[17]

Each of the four towers had an adjacent gun battery with parapets of sod work and stone platforms for the guns. The armament of each battery comprised two 24-pounder SBML guns on traversing platforms that had been made locally in Cork. The Cathcart Tower was the only tower to be armed with a mortar battery of two 13-in (330-mm) Land Service (LS) mortars mounted on iron beds and wooden platforms in the glacis. Behind each battery there was a stone-built magazine and a stone building to provide shelter for the gun crews. Immediately adjacent to Towers Nos. 2 and 3 there were also two small buildings used as Ordnance stores.

Despite all the difficulties of supervision and provision of materials and supplies work on the towers and batteries continued apace. By 2nd February 1805 Brigadier General Freeman, the Deputy Barrack Master General, had received the report that 'Four towers with casemates, one battery with Defensible Guardhouse and one Officer's Barrack situated on Bere Island are ready'.[18] This is a somewhat puzzling statement as only the Cathcart Tower is known to have been casemated and the only plan of the Manly tower, which was demolished in 1897, depicts a structure without a casemate.[19]

The original estimate for the construction of the Bere Island towers was £21,000 and that sum had originally been allocated by Major General Eyre Coote, the General Officer Commanding the Cork District, but by 1807 that total had increased to over £31,000 and in 1808 Brigadier General Fisher estimated that a further £13,500 would be needed to complete the works though this sum seems to have also included the cost of additional garrison buildings built subsequently. These included an officer's barrack, soldier's barrack, hospital, Engineer's house, Master Gunner's house and Commissary's house. This meant that a total of £45,000 had been expended on the Bere Island works and when Fisher requested a further £7,000 for further repairs Chief Secretary Pole insisted on a Board of Inquiry. When the Board assembled in 1809 Fisher pointed out that the difficulties of building on Bere Island were such that he believed no judgement could be made as to whether or not monies had been wasted and it would appear that the findings of the Board were inconclusive.[20] By 1809 the works on Bere Island had been transferred to the Board of Ordnance which had reluctantly agreed, after a lengthy and protracted negotiation, to take over the land and the maintenance of the towers, batteries and

buildings from the local District commander.

Over the years there was some criticism of the construction and siting of the towers and batteries. There were constant complaints that the towers were damp necessitating the provision of a winter fuel allowance throughout each summer and the siting of the towers was criticised by no less an authority than the Duke of Wellington himself. In 1806 Sir Arthur Wellesley, as Wellington was known at that time, was Chief Secretary when he visited Bantry Bay and inspected the work on Bere Island. His opinion was: 'The Towers are on very high ground and I am very doubtful if they would entirely answer the purpose of completely defending the anchorage'.[21] The criticism was probably not entirely fair as only Tower No. 4 at Ardagh stood on very high ground and it was clearly designed to prevent an enemy force occupying the high ground and attacking Lawrence Cove. The Manly and Cathcart Towers (Towers Nos. 1 and 2) had the role of defending the anchorage and Tower No. 3 at Clochlan was sited to prevent a landing on the southern shore close to Lawrence Cove.

The Later Years

The Bere Island towers were always a problem for the Board of Ordnance and by 1829 the batteries were described as being 'in a state of dilapidation, though the towers and masonry buildings were in a tolerable state.'[22] The main problem, however, was the remoteness of the island since it was 44 miles (70km) from the nearest Engineer office and, as a result, difficult and costly to get to, because Royal Engineers officers could claim travelling allowance. In fact, in 1831 the Commanding Royal Engineer in Cork complained that it took eight days travelling from Cork to inspect the Bantry Bay defences. It was also an unpopular station for the men manning the defences so the decision was taken to leave two pensioners in charge of the works on Bere Island.

In 1879 a Colonel Wray reported on the defences of Bantry and described the existing works of defence as being entirely out of date and useless for their intended purpose.[23] However the pensioners continued as caretakers of the towers until 1883 when the Defence Committee recommended that all War Office leasehold property on Bere Island should be given up. The land was surrendered to the owners in 1884 with the concurrence of the Admiralty as it did not appear probable that the defence of Berehaven would become necessary in the future and the appreciable sum of money involved in the rent and maintenance could thus be saved.

As so often happened when decisions were taken to give up coastal defence positions this decision was quickly reversed. Although the Admiralty had originally agreed to give up Berehaven as a defended anchorage in 1889 the changing political climate on the continent of Europe led their Lordships to review their position regarding Berehaven. There suddenly seemed a possibility of Britain having to face a hostile European power, either France or Germany, and Berehaven in the south west of Ireland and Lough Swilly in the north west now both seemed desirable harbours of refuge for merchant vessels approaching the United Kingdom from the western Atlantic.

In 1889 Rear Admiral Sir George Tryon wrote to the War Office to advise of the Admiralty's changed position and recommending that Berehaven and Lough Swilly should now be re-fortified with modern batteries mounting the latest breech-loading guns. In response to Admiral Tryon's letter the Royal Artillery and Royal Engineers Works Committee visited Berehaven and inspected the old defences and in a report dated 18th July 1889 had concluded that: 'The Martello towers erected at the beginning of the century on Bear [sic] Island, remain in fairly good repair and the old earthworks which still exist could be adapted to modern requirements without much difficulty'.[24] The committee recommended that both entrances to the anchorage should be defended and that two 6-in (152-mm) BL guns and one 4.7-in (120-mm) QF gun should be mounted on the site of the Manly Tower at Lonehort Point to defend the eastern entrance. It was proposed that one of the 6-in (152-mm) BL guns should be mounted on the Martello tower itself which would be reduced in height and the other two guns mounted on the site of Battery No.1 nearby. Two 4.7-in (120-mm) QF guns

Figure 1.12: Ardagh Tower (Tower No.4), Bere Island. This tower, which resembles the Addaya Tower on Minorca, has recently been refurbished. The ruins of the barrack block can be seen on the left.(*Author's photograph*).

Figure 1.13: Clochlan Tower (Tower No.3), Bere Island. This tower was used until 1938 by the British Army as the Port War Signal Station for Berehaven. (*Author's photograph*).

were proposed for the defence of the western entrance.

This level of armament would probably have been sufficient to defend Berehaven in its role as a 'Harbour of Refuge' for merchant vessels. However, the Joint Naval and Military Committee had a greater role in mind for the Berehaven anchorage. This committee was of the view that Berehaven should become a base for a Royal Navy squadron to be stationed there as well as being a 'Harbour of Refuge' and a coaling station.

The new plan involved the construction of two new forts at Rerrin and Lonehort to mount heavier 9.2-in (233-mm) BL guns as well as a number of 6-in (152-mm) BL guns as had been originally proposed together with an infantry redoubt at Rerrin. The construction of the new fort at Lonehort Point involved the demolition of the Manly Tower (Tower No.1) while the new infantry redoubt at Rerrin was to be built on the site of the Cathcart Tower (Tower No.2). The tower itself was demolished but much of the glacis was retained as were the counterscarp gallery and the magazine. The counterscarp gallery and magazine were re-used as stores, an office, telephone rooms and a machine-gun and small-arms ammunition store. A new single-storey accommodation building was built in

an area where the glacis had been levelled and a loop-holed wall built on top. A new fire control post was built on top of the glacis and in 1904 one of two Position-finding cells was built on top of the redoubt and the Rerrin redoubt then became the main head-quarters for the defences of Berehaven.

In 1891 it was proposed to move the Port War Signal Station to Bere Island but negotiations on the lease of the Martello tower at Clochlan (Tower No.3) were drawn out and it was not until 1909 that the War Office offer of a rent of £10 per annum was accepted. The tower then became the Port War Signal Station for Berehaven and a small accommo-dation hut and a semaphore mast were built close to the tower. The tower continued in that role until 1938 when the Treaty Port of Berehaven was returned to the government of Eire. Today Tower No.3 remains together with the concrete base of the semaphore mast and the foundations of the accom-modation hut. Sadly, the tower is in rather poor condition but can still be visited by anyone of a reasonably adventurous nature. However, Tower No.4 at Ardagh has been refurbished and now can be visited by anyone using the Beara Way which passes close to the tower and which is now one of the major features of this spectacular walk.

Chapter 2

—·—

THE DUBLIN TOWERS

In his report of July 1802 Colonel William Twiss RE laid down the priorities as he saw them for the defence of Ireland and the first and foremost priority was the defence of Dublin. Twiss had been concerned primarily with the landward defence of the city but in December 1803, with the failed rising of that year in Dublin still fresh in the mind of the government, there were intelligence reports of another planned French invasion. Since a French invasion force was being assembled around Boulogne such reports could not be disregarded and it was clear that the coast north and south of Dublin would be particularly vulnerable to a French landing should an invasion fleet succeed in evading the Royal Navy.

In January 1804 Lord Cathcart received a request from the Lord Lieutenant that steps should be taken, with the least possible delay, to fortify the coast immediately to the north and south of Dublin by building towers and batteries. These were to be constructed as 'Field Works' under the direct authority of the Commander-in-Chief rather than the Board of Ordnance but despite this fact and the request that the matter should be put in hand without the least delay work did not start until July.

This delay may have been the result of the requirement to obtain a detailed estimate of the cost of construction of the towers and batteries and perhaps because of a certain reluctance on the part of Colonel Fisher, the Commanding Royal Engineer in Dublin, to divert his limited engineer resources to superintending this major project which had not been approved by the Board of Ordnance. However, on 29th May Lord Cathcart was authorised by Mr Secretary Wickham to 'take steps to secure those parts of the coast between Drogheda and Wexford which Rear Admiral Whitshed suggests could be used by an enemy as landing places'.[1] Rear Admiral Whitshed RN had been despatched to Ireland in 1803 to act as naval adviser to the Lord Lieutenant and was subsequently responsible for the construction of a line of signal towers along most of the Irish coastline.

Lord Cathcart endeavoured, as we have seen, to obtain the services of his protegee, Captain Birch RE, and there seems every likelihood that the latter was responsible for the design of many, if not all, of the towers built to defend Dublin. Initially Birch did not approve of the plan for the Dublin towers advising Lord Cathcart that it would be better to fortify the capital since the coast defences could easily be turned further north or south.[2]

However, Birch's argument did not prevail and it would appear that Colonel Fisher carried out the preliminary reconnaissance on which the siting of the towers and batteries was subsequently based while Birch, who had the experience of building similar towers on Minorca, designed the towers. This is most likely since there is a very close resemblance between the design of the towers on Minorca, in particular the Addaya tower, and that of the Dublin towers. Fisher planned to construct a total of twenty six towers and ten batteries, twelve towers, numbered 1 to 12, north of Dublin and fourteen towers and ten batteries, numbered 1 to 16 along the coast south of the city. Battery No.5 and Battery No.8 on the south coast were the two batteries built without an adjoining tower.

The twenty six towers were of two types, a standard

Figure 2.1: Ireland's Eye Island tower. This was one of the four large 'double' towers built to mount two heavy guns and the only 'double' tower built north of Dublin. (*Author's photograph*).

design with an external base diameter of 38ft (11.6m) and a height of approximately 30ft (9.2m) and a larger tower some 50ft (15.3m) in external base diameter and with a height of approximately 30 – 32ft (9.2 – 9.8m). A total of twenty two towers were built to the standard design, eleven south of Dublin and eleven to the north. Three of the larger towers were built on the south coast and a single large tower to the north. These larger towers were known in contemporary documents as 'double' towers as each mounted two heavy guns and the design of these towers was to be peculiar to Ireland and some colonies. The northern towers were frequently sited at some considerable distance from the next tower as the aim was to defend the likely landing places north of Dublin. South of the city the towers were sited much closer together in order to enable each tower to support those on either side of it.

A number of the northern towers were the first of the Dublin towers to be built, and these were the towers at Sutton, Howth Hill, Ireland's Eye Island, Malahide, Portrane, Rush, Shenick's Island, Red Island and Balbriggan. They were constructed of rendered rubble masonry while the southern towers were of granite in regular ashlar courses. Each tower, except the one on Dalkey Island, had two storeys, the ground floor containing the magazine and a store

with the first floor providing the living accommodation. A return giving the available accommodation in the towers submitted in the middle of the nineteenth century showed that the northern towers had accommodation for sixteen men and the southern towers twelve men, though the Dalkey Island tower was reported as having no accommodation at all. In that case the accommodation for the gunners of the tower and the adjacent battery was provided in a small adjoining barrack building. In none of the Dublin towers was accommodation shown for an officer.

All the Dublin towers had a bomb-proof roof supporting the gun platform but none had a central pillar, as was to be provided in the English towers, and, as originally built, there were no windows except in the case of the Dalkey Island tower which was provided with a single window. However, there were a number of light shafts set at an angle in the wall and sloping upwards. Access internally between each floor, except in the Dalkey Island tower, was by way of a stone staircase which was built into the thickness of the wall. In addition, in a number of towers there was a shaft leading from the first floor up to the gun platform through which powder and shot could be passed to the gun. In Tower No.7 south of Dublin this shaft was set into a recess in the wall above the door.

Most of the towers had a projecting *machicoulis* at

Figure 2.2: Dalkey Island Tower. This tower was unusual in that entrance was by ladder through an aperture in the parapet. The original aperture, now blocked up, can be seen immediately above the dark line on the side of the tower. The lower door is a later addition. *(Author's photograph)*.

parapet level over the doorway but the Williamstown tower had a projecting parapet supported by two continuous courses of corbels. In place of a *machicoulis* there were two openings in the corbel courses supporting the parapet, one on each side of the door, to enable musketry fire to be brought to bear on an enemy attacking the entrance. It is also possible that Tower No.3 at Corke Abbey south of Dublin was similar to the Williamstown tower in having a projecting parapet without a *machicoulis*. The tower was destroyed by sea erosion in 1865 but there is an early sketch in the National Gallery of Ireland that appears to show a similar parapet. The tower on Ireland's Eye Island had a double string

Bathing Place, Howth

Figure 2.3: An early 20th century postcard showing the tower on the Hill of Howth. *(Author's collection)*.

Figure 2.4: The Williamstown tower south of Dublin. This tower was one of the three 'Double' towers built to defend the coast south of Dublin. Today the tower stands less than its original height due to land infill. (*Author's photograph*).

course at the base of the parapet and had a large *machicoulis* supported by seven corbels.

The standard tower was designed to mount one

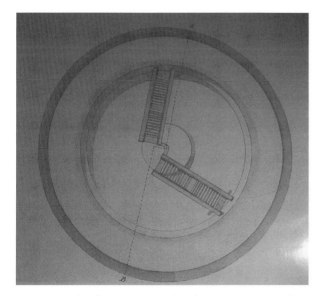

Figure 2.5: Plan for a mounting of two heavy guns on a single rear pivot. This was a mounting developed by Colonel Benjamin Fisher RE when Commanding Royal Engineer in Dublin and subsequently only used in Ireland and a number of towers overseas. (*TNA MR 1/1771*).

heavy gun on the gun platform, but the four larger towers mounted two heavy guns. The guns on the larger 'double' towers had their guns mounted using a single rear-mounted central pivot, a system that, initially, was unique to towers in Ireland and which was never used in England, though some towers overseas had a similar mounting. The northern towers were armed with a single 24-pounder SBML gun, except the tower on Ireland's Eye Island which mounted two. To the south the standard towers mounted the lighter 18-pounder SBML gun but the three 'double' towers, at Williamstown, Sandymount and Dalkey Island, each mounted two of the heavier 24-pounder guns. The ten batteries mounted between three and five 24-pounder guns each and those at Sandycove and Kingstown were provided with two 10-in (254-mm) mortars. Each battery was defended by a loopholed wall and had a small stone building as a store and a stone-built magazine.

As with most Martello towers entry to the Dublin towers was by means of a door at first-floor level opening directly into the accommodation area at first floor level. In the Bullock tower, however, the doorway passage is unusual as it is constructed in the form of a dogleg, so providing additional protection.

Although entry to the towers was usually at first floor level this was not the case in the Dalkey Island tower. This tower was the exception as it had only one storey with the floor only a few feet above the ground and under which was a small cistern. Entrance to the tower is shown in a section and plan of the tower dated 1868 as being through the parapet wall, and the Dalkey Island tower is the only Irish tower known to have been entered in this manner.[3]

The interior of the tower was also unusual in that the single chamber was divided into two unequal parts, the smaller forming two magazines separated by a wall and with a door into each. The tower had no machicolation because of its parapet entrance, but built into the thickness of the wall there was a shaft, similar to those in the towers on Minorca, running directly from the parapet to the chamber and which was used to move powder and shot to the guns. Communication between the chamber and the gun platform was by means of the usual staircase within the wall of the tower. All the towers north of Dublin and six towers south of Dublin at Bray, Maghera Point, Bullock, Sandycove, Williamstown and Sandymount which were unsupported by batteries were provided with a shot furnace built into the parapet of the gun platform.

Colonel Fisher originally estimated the cost of each of the Dublin towers at £1,800 but by December 1805 the total cost for the Dublin Bay towers and batteries was estimated at £64,082, an average cost of

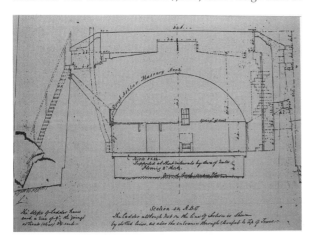

Figure 2.6: Section of the tower on Dalkey Island. (*Military Archives, Dublin*).

Figure 2.7: This photograph shows the ammunition shaft in Ireland's Eye Island tower that enabled ammunition to be passed from the first floor to the gun platform through the *machicoulis*. (*Author's photograph*).

almost £2,300 per tower. However, the final cost came to over £100,000. This sum included the cost of roads to the towers and two small harbours at Bullock and on Dalkey Island for the Ordnance boats serving the Dalkey Island and Ireland's Eye Island towers. In addition there was the maintenance cost over a seven year period but even so it would seem that huge cost overruns were not unknown in the building industry even in the early nineteenth century![4]

With the end of the Napoleonic War the towers were retained as part of the defences of Dublin but were only manned by Invalid Gunners or pensioners. A number of the Dublin towers were subsequently taken over by the Revenue Preventative Service, the forerunner of the Coastguard. North of Dublin, in the 1830s, these included Tower No.2 at Howth Hill; Tower No.3 on Ireland's Eye Island; Tower No.7 at Portrane; Tower No.9 at Drumanagh; and Tower No.12 at Balbriggan. Subsequently Tower No.8 at Rush and Tower No. 11 on Red Island were also used later by the Coastguard. South of Dublin the towers were Tower No. 2 at Bray Head; Tower No.6 at Loughlinstown; Tower No.11 at Sandycove; Tower No.12 at Glasthule (until its demolition in 1848); Tower No.13 at Dun Laoghaire Harbour and Tower No.15 at Williamstown.[5]

In 1827 a request to the Board of Ordnance to

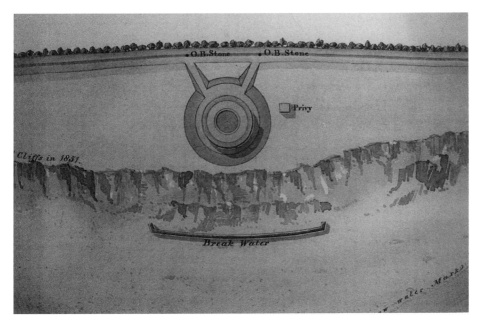

Figure 2.8: Plan of the tower at Maghera Point, Tower No.4 south of Dublin. This tower was threatened by sea erosion in the 1840s and a breakwater built to attempt to save the tower and an associated battery to the south. (*TNA WO 78/4760*).

Figure 2.9: An early watercolour showing a section of the Dublin and Kingstown Railway with the Williamstown tower in the background. The picture clearly shows how the railway cut off the tower from the sea. (*Author's collection*).

relinquish Towers Nos. 12 and 13 was refused on the grounds that the 'utility of these towers has been greatly increased as a result of the formation of the Pier and Harbour at Kingstown'[6] However, in 1836 the Board of Ordnance sold Tower No.13 and its adjacent battery for £1,700 to allow the completion of an extension to the recently constructed Dublin to Kingstown railway. The sale of Tower No.13 was a precedent which permitted the Board of Ordnance in 1848 to negotiate with the Board of Works the exchange of the Glasthule tower and battery for houses in Great Ship Street in Dublin. The tower was subsequently purchased in 1854 by the Commissioners for Kingstown Harbour and the tower demolished. In 1862 most of the towers were occupied

by Invalid Gunners and their families and of the eight remaining batteries supporting towers south of Dublin only three, Dalkey Island, Sandycove and Tara Hill, were still armed. The remainder were described on plans as either being dismantled or in ruins while both the towers at Dun Laoghaire had been demolished.

By 1885 the Martello towers were considered to be obsolete as defensive structures and a report stated 'They are without exception useless for purposes of defence and the sites are no longer required for the modern fortifications required for Dublin Bay'.[7] The report noted that the Coastguard occupied the Portrane tower north of Dublin and Tower No.11 south of Dublin while some towers were let at small rents to private individuals and it recommended that

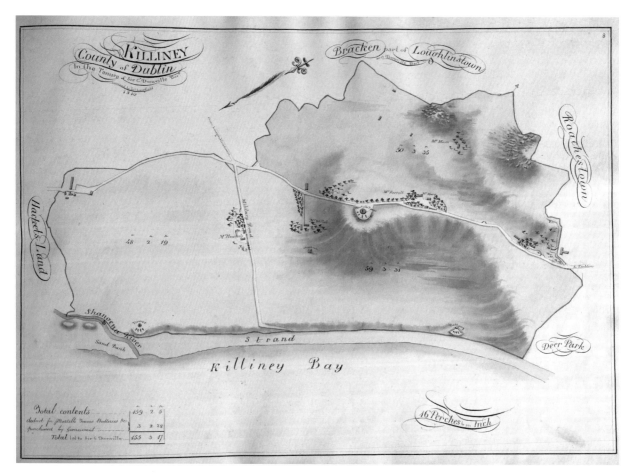

Figure 2.10: A map of Killiney Bay, Dublin showing the Tara Hill tower (Tower No.7 South) sited on high ground to the rear of, and between, the Loughlinstown tower (Tower No.6 South) and the Limekiln Battery. The tower on Tara Hill was sited to defend the high ground overlooking Killiney beach rather than to engage ships. *(Niall O'Donoghue)*

Dalkey Battery and the other towers should be disarmed and disposed of. Interestingly, the armament of Dalkey Island battery was shown in the report as being three 64-pounder RML guns. As such it was the only tower or battery defending Dublin, other than the Pigeon House Fort, ever to be armed with rifled guns until the Second World War although similar guns were proposed for the towers at Sutton, Bullock, Seapoint and Sandycove but these were never mounted. In 1895 it was proposed that a single 6-in (152-mm) BL gun should be mounted on Tower No.11 at Sandycove but the proposal was never implemented.

During the Second World War a 12-pounder 12-cwt QF gun without a shield was mounted in the old Sandycove Battery to act as the examination battery for the port of Dublin and the Sandycove tower was used as the battery observation post. To the north of Dublin the Rush tower was used by the Coastwatching Service and a concrete OP was built on the gun platform. With the end of the Second World War little interest was taken in the towers and they were allowed to deteriorate. Recently, however, a number have been converted into private residences with varying degrees of success since, sadly, the historical integrity of the tower has not always been taken into account. Two towers, at Howth and Sandycove have been adapted as museums and one, No.7 at Tara Hill south of Dublin, has been completely restored to its original condition by a private owner, Niall O'Donoghue. The Dublin Martello towers are now protected as architectural monuments which are part of the country's architectural heritage and a survey has recently been carried out to identify their importance.

The Northern Towers

No.1, Red Island, Sutton. A standard tower with a four-corbelled *machicoulis*. The original armament was a single 24-pounder SBML gun. It defended an important approach to Dublin city for smaller vessels. It has now been converted into a private residence with a sun room on the gun platform. In 1875 it was proposed to mount one 64-pounder RML gun in place of the 24-pounder gun but the proposal was never implemented.

Figure 2.11: Tower No.1 north of Dublin at Sutton Creek. This is one of a number of the Dublin towers now converted into private residences. (*Author's photograph*).

No.2, Howth Hill. A standard tower with a five-corbelled *machicoulis*. The original armament was a single 24-pounder SBML gun. In 1854 the tower became a cable station for the Irish end of the new telegraph cable between Britain and Ireland and, in the early years of the twentieth century, was subsequently used for experiments in wireless telegraphy by the American inventor Lee de Forrest and the Marconi Company. Today the tower has been restored and is in use as the Vintage Radio Museum.

No.3, Ireland's Eye Island. A large 'double' tower on the north-western tip of the island. It has a large seven-corbelled *machicoulis* and was armed with two rear-pivot mounted 24-pounder SBML guns. It was completed by 31st August 1805 and sited to command the approaches to Howth Harbour. It now stands un-restored but in good condition.

No.4, Portmarnock. A standard tower which was armed with a single 24-pounder SBML gun on a wooden traversing platform. This platform was replaced with an iron platform and carriage in 1847. The tower is now a private residence and has been substantially altered by the addition of a castellated third storey.

No.5, Robswall, Malahide. A standard tower originally armed with a single 24-pounder SBML gun. The tower was completed by 31st August 1805 and in 1847 the armament of the tower was improved by the provision of a new iron traversing platform and carriage. In 1908 the tower was sold by the War Office and it was converted into a private residence in 1911 to an Arts and Crafts design by the architect Frederick Hicks and now has a conical roof with a tall chimney stack and dormer windows. It is surrounded by a castellated wall and is scarcely recognisable as a Martello tower.

No.6, Balcarrick, Donabate. A standard tower with

a five-corbelled *machicoulis* which was originally armed with a single 24-pounder SBML gun. The tower was sold in 1909 and in the 1950s a later owner appears to have built a wall on the landward side of the gun platform, possibly part of a sunroom. The tower is now derelict.

No.7, Portrane. A standard tower with a large seven-corbelled *machicoulis*. It was armed with a single 24-pounder SBML gun and completed by 31st August 1805. The tower was used by the Preventative Water Guard and the Coast Guard between 1826 and the 1860s. The tower has now been restored and converted into a private residence with additional accommodation built around the base of the tower.

No.8, Rush. A standard tower armed with a 24-pounder SBML gun with a five-corbelled *machicoulis*. During the 'Emergency' (the Second World War) a coast-watching post was built on the gun platform of the tower. It is now privately owned but in appearance has not been substantially altered.

No.9, Drumanagh. A standard tower with a five-corbelled machicoulis and armed with a 24-pounder

Figure 2.12: Tower No.6 at Balcarrick, north of Dublin. This tower is now derelict. The door of the tower is now close to ground level due to the rise in the level of the sand dunes. *(Photograph Andrew Clements).*

Figure 2.13: Drumanagh tower north of Dublin. This tower mounted a single 24-pounder SB gun and the *machicoulis* over the door can be clearly seen in this photograph. There is a clear resemblance to the earlier towers on Minorca (*Author's photograph*).

SBML gun. It stands on Drumanagh headland and was sited to defend Rush Strand and the pier at Drumanagh Point. The tower was occupied by the Preventative Water Guard and the Coast Guard between 1821 and 1857. It now stands in a derelict condition.

No.10, Shenick's Island. A standard tower with a five-corbelled *machicoulis* that was armed with a 24-pounder SBML gun. It has a shot furnace and the central pivot for the gun is mounted on a circular granite block. There are grooves cut in the stone of the gun platform that lead to a hole which allows

Tower and Baths, Balbriggan

Figure 2.14: An early 20th century postcard view of Tower No.12 north at Balbriggan north of Dublin. The tower is now derelict. (*Author's collection*).

rainwater to flow into a 350-gallon water tank in the basement. The tower is un-restored but in a reasonable condition.

No.11, Red Island, Skerries. A standard tower with a five-corbelled *machicoulis*. It was armed with a 24-pounder SBML gun on a wooden traversing platform that was replaced by an iron platform and carriage in 1847. The current ground-floor entrance is not original. The tower has previously been used as a café, private residence, part of a holiday camp and more recently as a local council store. It has now been refurbished and has been made accessible to the public.

No.12, Balbriggan. A standard tower armed with a 24-pounder gun constructed to defend the pier and cove at Balbriggan. It was occupied by the Preventive Water Guard, a forerunner of the Coast Guard in 1823 and subsequently used by the Coast Guard between 1870 and 1909. The tower is now derelict and in deteriorating condition, the parapet and the *machicoulis* having disappeared in the middle of the last century. Today the tower is owned by Fingal County Council.

The Southern Towers

No.1, Bray Head. Standard tower armed with a single 18-pounder SBML gun which was replaced with a 24-pounder gun in 1853. The tower supported a battery of four 24-pounder SB guns immediately in front of the tower with a small guardhouse adjacent to the tower but separate from it. The tower was demolished in 1884 by the Bray Town Commissioners and the stone used in the building of the sea wall.

No.2, Bray Point. Also known as Mount Park this is a standard tower with a four-corbelled *machicoulis*. It was originally armed with a single 18-pounder SBML gun and supported a battery of four 24-pounder guns. The original gun was replaced with a 24-pounder gun in 1853. By 1859 a guard house and a house for an officer had been built one on each side of the tower. It is now a private residence and one of the tower's previous owners was the singer Bono of the rock band U2.

No.3, Corke Abbey, Bray. Standard tower armed with a single 18-pounder SBML gun which was replaced with a 24-pounder gun in 1853. In an early

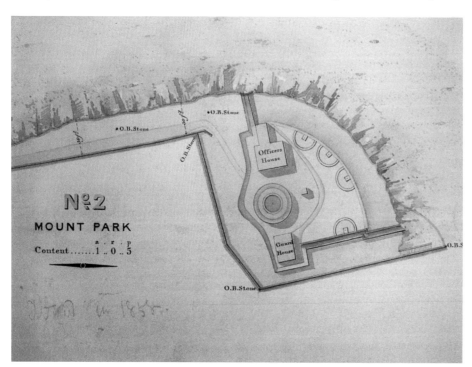

Figure 2.15: Plan of Mount Park Tower, Bray (Tower No.2) and its associated battery south of Dublin. The battery was armed with four 24-pounder SB guns. (*TNA WO 78/4760*).

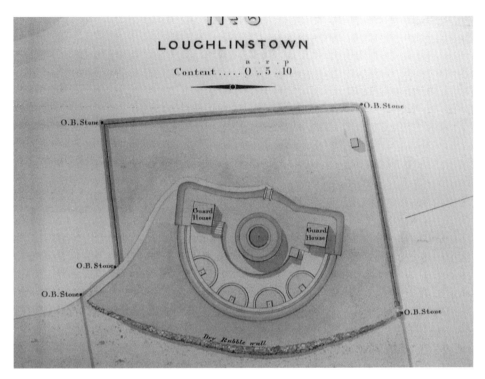

Figure 2.16: Plan of the Loughlinstown tower (No.6 South) showing the battery for four guns and, unusually, two small guard houses one on each flank. (*TNA WO 78/4760*)

sketch held by the National Gallery of Ireland the tower appears to resemble the Williamstown tower in having a projecting parapet rather than a *machicoulis*. The tower was destroyed as a result of sea erosion in the 1880s.

No.4, Maghera Point, Shankill. Standard tower armed with a single 18-pounder SBML gun replaced by a 24-pounder gun in 1853. It was surrounded by a ditch and unusually it supported two batteries, each of two 24-pounder guns, known, respectively, as the East and West Batteries. The tower was demolished by Royal Engineers in 1906, the structure having become dangerous due to sea erosion despite the construction of breakwaters on the beach in front of the tower and the south battery.

Battery No.5, Shanganagh, Killiney. No tower was built to support this battery of four 24-pounder SBML guns though the construction of a tower to mount one 24-pounder and one 8-in howitzer was proposed in 1811 with an estimated cost of £2,907.5s.1d but the tower was never built. The battery was sited to scour the beach and co-operate with No.6 in defence

of that part of the bay. It suffered from erosion and the Board of Ordnance approved of it being dismantled in December 1812. Parts of the battery were demolished in 1816 but the angled, loopholed defensive walls, the guard house and magazine still remain.

No.6, Loughlinstown, Killiney. A standard tower originally armed with a single 18-pounder SBML gun and associated with an adjacent battery of four 24-pounder guns sited to defend Killiney beach. The gun on the tower was replaced with a 24-pounder gun in 1853. Unusually, the tower has a three-corbelled *machicoulis*. In 1859 a guard house was constructed on each side of the tower. The tower was reconstructed in 1971 by Victor Enoch who, regrettably, built two additional floors on top of the gun platform. However, the tower itself remains reasonably intact though other structures have been built in close proximity to the tower.

No.7, Tara Hill, Killiney. A standard tower with an interesting three-corbelled *machicoulis* consisting of two large double corbels one each side of a central single corbel. It was originally armed with a single

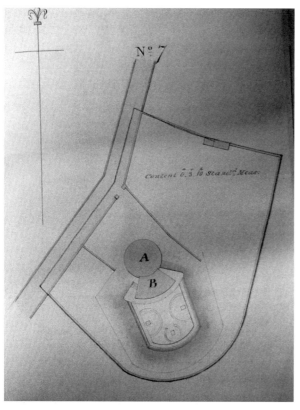

Figure 2.17: Plan of the Tara Hill tower (Tower No.7) and battery south of Dublin. *(TNA WO 78/4760)*.

18-pounder SBML gun and supported a battery at the foot of the tower of three 24-pounder guns. It was sited on the hill in order to support the towers on the shoreline and to provide *enfilade* fire. The guns in the battery were replaced by heavier 32-pounder guns and the gun in the tower with a 24-pounder gun in 1853. The guns of the battery were mounted behind a low parapet and glacis and a unique feature of this tower is the single-storey guardroom built on to the front of the tower. This is a low building with a sloping slate roof and seven musketry loopholes covering the *terreplein* of the battery. This tower was the only tower to be provided with such a guardhouse and this was probably because there was insufficient space available to build a detached guardhouse. In 2008 the tower was completely restored by Niall O'Donoghue who installed a replica 24-pounder gun and traversing platform on the gun platform.

Battery No.8, Limekiln, Killiney. This was a battery for four 24-pounder SBML guns without a tower but with a guardhouse, magazine and store and sited to defend Killiney beach. The battery was largely demolished to make way for the construction of the railway in 1854-56.

Figure 2.18: Tower No.7 (South) at Tara Hill. This tower has been completely restored to its original state by the present owner. *(Author's photograph)*.

Figure 2.19: The Tara Hill tower now fully refurbished. The picture shows a re-enactor in the Napoleonic period uniform of the 88th Foot (The Connaught Rangers). (*Author's photograph*)

Figure 2.20: Reproduction 24-pounder Blomefield gun on the gun platform of the Tara Hill tower. (*Author's photograph*).

Figure 2.21: The Tara Hill tower, south of Dublin; the picture shows the firing of the replica 24-pounder smooth-bore gun now mounted on the gun platform of the tower. *(Author's photograph)*

No.9, Dalkey Island. This is a 'double' tower and is still in very good condition. It was armed with two 24-pounder SBML guns and supported a battery of three similar guns which were later replaced by three 32-pounder guns and then by three 64-pounder RML guns. There is no *machicoulis* over the door of the tower and the battery is a fully enclosed work standing some distance from the tower and constructed of granite ashlar. Accommodation for the gunners of the battery was in a separate barrack building. The tower and battery appear to be sited to prevent boats using Dalkey Sound and to provide *enfilade* fire against any attempt to land troops at the northern end of Killiney Bay.

No.10, Bullock (Bartra Rock). A standard tower with a five-corbelled *machicoulis* that was armed with

a single 18-pounder SBML gun. This gun was removed in 1853 and a single 8-in (203-mm) SB shell gun installed in its place. The tower is privately owned and has been restored as a residence.

No.11, Sandycove. A standard tower with a five-corbelled *machicoulis*, this tower was originally armed with a single 18-pounder SBML gun. This gun was replaced by a 32-pounder gun in 1853. A large battery for five 24-pounder guns and two 10-in mortars was located on the rocks overlooking the present 'Forty Foot' bathing place not far from the tower. These guns were replaced in 1853 by one 68-pounder SBML gun and five 8-in (203-mm) SB shell guns. A proposal to mount a 64-pounder RML gun on the tower was never implemented and the tower and battery were abandoned in 1897. During the Second World War a 12-pounder QF gun was mounted on the old battery *terreplein*. The tower was used for a period in the 19th century by the Coastguard and was rented in 1904 by the War Office to the Irish poet Oliver St John Gogarty for a rent of £8 per annum. Gogarty served as the inspiration for Buck Milligan in James Joyce's novel *Ulysses*. The tower was sold in 1954, restored and converted into the James Joyce Museum.

No.12, Glasthule, Dun Laoghaire. A standard tower with a *machicoulis* and armed with a single 18-pounder SBML gun. The tower supported a battery of three 24-pounder guns and two 10-in (254-mm) mortars. The tower was disarmed in 1825 and five years later it was taken over by the Preventative Water Guard. In 1848 the tower and land were exchanged for houses in Great Ship Street in Dublin and in 1854 the tower was purchased by the Commissioners for Kingstown Harbour and demolished some years later.

No.13, Dun Laoghaire Harbour. A standard tower armed with a single 18-pounder SBML gun. It supported a battery of four 24-pounder guns and two 10-in (254mm) mortars. The tower stood on higher ground to the rear of the battery overlooking the old pier. The tower was demolished when the West Pier was built in the middle of the nineteenth century.

No.14, Seapoint. A standard tower with a five-corbelled *machicoulis* which was originally armed with a single 18-pounder SBML gun. In 1853 the 18-pounder gun was replaced by an 8-in (203-mm) SB shell gun but a later proposal to mount a RML gun on the tower was never implemented. The tower did not support a battery and was disarmed at the end of the nineteenth century. The tower was restored by the Genealogical Society of Ireland to be used as the Society's headquarters but proved to be too damp for the storage of its records. The tower has been further restored by the Dun Laoghaire-Rathdown County Council and today it is open to the public for conducted tours.

No.15, Williamstown, Blackrock. This tower was the only Dublin tower to have been constructed with a projecting parapet. It was a 'double' tower with no *machicoulis* but with two openings in the projecting parapet, one on each side of the door of the tower.

Figure 2.22: Sandycove tower. This tower is now the James Joyce Museum. (*Author's photograph*).

Figure 2.23: Tower No.14 at Seapoint, south of Dublin. This tower was restored some years ago and was used for some time by the Genealogical Society of Ireland to store the Society's archives. The tower proved too damp for this role and reverted to the Dun Laoghaire-Rathdown County Council that carried out further restoration and opened the tower to public viewing. (*Author's photograph*).

The tower resembled the tower built at Santandria, near Ciudadela on Minorca and the Cathcart Tower on Bere Island. The tower was originally armed with two 24-pounder SBML guns and, when first built, was surrounded by seawater at high tide and so was not supported by a battery. In 1818 Major General Fyers, the Commanding Royal Engineer in Dublin, reported that the tower 'which is one of our best' had been 'much injured from the heavy gales we had sometime ago'.[8] The tower was subsequently isolated from the sea when the railway was constructed in the 1840s and by a new drainage system which was installed in the 1870s. Although most Martello towers were provided with a privy in the grounds adjacent to the tower the Williamstown tower was one of only two Irish towers to have a privy built into the parapet. The tower was used for some years as a residence and the ground level around the tower was raised reducing the overall height of the tower. The basement has been filled with earth and the doorway is now at ground floor level. Until the 1990s the tower was used as a changing room by the Williamstown Football Club and is now owned by the Dun Laoghaire-Rathdown Council which intends to restore the tower.

No.16, Sandymount. A 'double' tower that was armed with two 24-pounder SBML guns but was not supported by a battery. It has a five-corbelled *machicoulis* and in the mid-nineteenth century a plan shows a yard and privy built on to the tower, though this tower, like the Williamstown tower, also had a privy built into the parapet. The tower was disarmed at the end of the nineteenth century when it was taken over and used as offices and as a tram terminus by the Dublin United Tramways Company. Subsequently the tower had a modern structure built on in place of the yard and a footpath was opened through the ground floor section of the tower in 1922. The ground floor structure previously housed a café which has closed and today the tower is being refurbished on the orders of the local council.

Chapter 3

THE TOWERS OF LOUGH SWILLY AND LOUGH FOYLE

Lough Swilly

The landing of French troops in Ireland under General Humbert in 1798 and the two other abortive attempts to invade in the same year led to the hasty fortification of Lough Swilly, one of the two major sea loughs that, five years later, Colonel Twiss of the Royal Engineers was to recommend should be fortified permanently. The importance of Lough Swilly as an anchorage for both Royal Navy and merchant ships was now appreciated by the Admiralty and the government in Ireland also appreciated that the lough was strategically important to an enemy as an approach to the important city of Londonderry.

The 1798 fortifications comprised two small forts at the entrance to the lough, the East Fort on Dunree Head and the West Fort on Knockalla Head. In addition, a number of sodwork batteries for one or two guns were built as 'Field Works' on both shores of the lough. The guns for these batteries and for the West Fort came from the French line-of-battle ship *Hoche* captured in October 1798 by Commodore Sir John Warren RN and his squadron off the mouth of Lough Swilly.

These field works remained the sole defences for the next ten years and although some work was carried out on the two forts the condition of the batteries deteriorated and by 1805 the Clerk of the Ordnance on an inspection tour of the north of Ireland reported: 'It is impossible, however, for any Common Observer to pass through the Batteries belonging to Lough Swilly without being struck by the disgraceful Manner in which they are constructed. As there is now a Committee of

Engineers in Ireland acting under immediate Order of the Master General I beg leave to recommend it to the Board to request his Lordship to direct the Gentlemen to examine and report upon the State of the Works at Lough Swilly'.[1]

The Committee of Engineers comprised Brigadier General Gother Mann RE (later to be Inspector General of Fortifications) and Lieutenant Colonel Robert D'Arcy RE and in August and September 1806 they inspected Lough Foyle and the fortifications along the shores of Lough Swilly. Their report was to result in a complete reconstruction of the defences of Lough Swilly and the construction, for the first time, of fortifications to defend Lough Foyle.

Improvement of the Lough Swilly defences was a long drawn out and tedious business. The Committee of Engineers proposed to reform the East and West forts by increasing the number of guns mounted in each fort. In addition, the temporary batteries at Macamish Point and Rathmullen on the western shore of the lough and Ned's Point and Inch Island on the eastern shore were each to have a tower mounting two guns and permanent batteries. At Ned's Point the battery was to be armed with four heavy guns, at Inch Island five heavy guns, and Rathmullen five heavy guns and two 10-in (254 mm) mortars. The battery at Macamish Point was to be armed with two 13-in (330-mm) mortars. However, this armament was subsequently changed to three 24-pounder SBML guns and one 8-in (203-mm) howitzer on the tower as mortars were regarded as being ill-suited to engaging moving targets, even those that moved comparatively slowly. Two 13-in

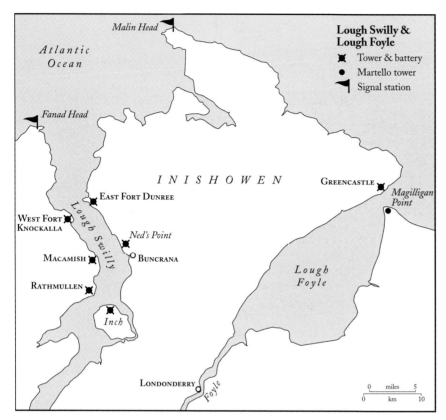

Figure 3.1: Towers of Lough Swilly and Lough Foyle. *(Martin Brown)*

Figure 3.2: The tower of Knockalla (West) Fort showing the *epaulement* added later to provide protection to the gunners from the fire of an enemy occupying the high ground to the rear of the fort. Dunree (East) Fort in the background. *(Author's photograph)*.

Figure 3.3: Sketch of Dunree (East) Fort at the entrance to Lough Swilly. The fort had a raised platform for two heavy guns rather than a Martello tower which, in fact, it resembled. *(TNA WO 78/4609)*.

(330-mm)mortars were added to the armament of both Rathmullen and Down of Inch batteries with those at Rathmullen replacing the two 10-in (254-mm)mortars originally proposed.

For three years the plans were considered by the Commanding Royal Engineer in Dublin and by the Board of Ordnance in London. Despite the apparent urgency of the work a debate continued concerning various details of the design of the towers. In October 1809 the Board of Ordnance was considering a proposal to erect square towers at the West Fort and the battery at Ned's Point but it was noted that a suggestion to surround each with a ditch would incur further expense.[2] Colonel Fisher, the Commanding Royal Engineer in Dublin, was also unhappy with the design for the entrance to the tower at Inch, pointing out that 'the side on which it is masked is the safest' and that 'loopholes devised in the tower by Colonel D'Arcy for the defence of the rear of the battery will be difficult to execute'.[3]

There was further delay in constructing the towers and batteries as Lough Swilly, like Bere Island, was inaccessible and there was reluctance on the part of contractors in Londonderry to tender for the work. Eventually a Mr Edgar successfully tendered for the contracts to build or rebuild the Lough Swilly forts

and batteries. Initially the plan was for each of the forts and batteries to have a circular tower to defend the landward side and act as a keep but in the final outcome only the two forts and two of the batteries were provided with Martello towers while the other two were defended by what were described as 'defensible guardhouses', or 'quadrangular towers', which will be described in a later chapter. These 'quadrangular towers' were proposed for the battery at Rathmullen and, at Ned's Point, a small promontory near Buncrana.

The East Fort 'tower' was not a tower as such but actually a circular stone gun platform built on the highest point within the walls of the fort and in some respects resembled the tower on Dalkey Island. The wall of the 'tower' varied in height between 26ft (8m) and 15ft (4.6m) owing to the irregular lay of the ground. The 'tower' had a small internal chamber and the gun platform, on which two 24-pounder SBML guns were mounted, was approached up a flight of stone steps leading directly to the parapet from the main fort rather than by means of the more usual ladder.

The design of the West Fort tower was based on that of the English east coast towers which mounted three guns on the gun platform but in the case of the West

Figure 3.4: Knockalla (West) Fort from the air. *(Dermot Rainey)*.

Fort tower only two guns were mounted as the position for the third was taken up by the covered exit to the internal staircase. The tower was cam-shaped in plan and at its widest it was 65ft (20m) and about 30ft (9.2m) high and had a central pillar supporting the bomb-proof roof. Work on the tower did not commence until after 1812 and the tower was badly constructed resulting in its collapse in 1815. The Assistant Engineer at Lough Swilly, Captain William Smith, evidently blamed the contractor, Mr Edgar, as he commented at the bottom of the sketch he made of the collapsed tower: 'Sketch of the Tower at Knockalla Fort, made after the fall thereof in order to show the infamous work made therein by the contractor, the fall having been foretold by Captain Wm.A.Smith Assistant Engineer prior to the same in 1815'.[4]

The towers of both forts had an *epaulement* built on the landward side of the parapet to defend the gunners from musketry fire from an enemy occupying a hill that overlooked each fort. It would appear that these *epaulements* were later additions to the towers. Indeed, the East Fort on Dunree Head had long been known to be vulnerable to a landward attack because of Dunree Hill which overlooked the fort. In 1805, before the rebuilding of the fort, a plan had been submitted to the Inspector General of Fortifications for a tower mounting one heavy gun on a traversing platform to be built on the summit of the hill. The tower was never built and until the very end of the century, in the 1890s when an infantry redoubt was built on the hill, the fort remained vulnerable to the fire of an enemy force occupying the top of Dunree Hill.

The tower at Macamish Point on the western shore of the lough was eventually built to the same design as that of the Dublin 'double' towers. It was a large circular tower of cut stone on which two heavy 24-pounder SB guns were mounted using a single rear pivot instead of the 8-in (203-mm) howitzer originally proposed. The tower stood on a rocky headland at the rear of the three-gun battery surrounded by the sea on three sides and so securing the gorge of the battery. The only approach was along the headland and across a small drawbridge which allowed access over a deep gulley. Entrance to the tower itself was through the usual door at first-floor level and there

was a five-corbelled *machicoulis* over the door. The
role of the tower and battery was to provide crossing
fire with the fort built on Ned's Point on the eastern
shore of the lough, a mile (1.6km) north of the small
town of Buncrana.

At Inch Island the tower, which also secured the
gorge of the battery, resembled the tower of the West
Fort at Knockalla, being cam-shaped in plan like the
English East coast towers and mounting two 5½-in
(140-mm) howitzers. Unlike the English towers there
was an *epaulement* built at the rear of the gun platform
in a similar fashion to the Knockalla tower and nine
musket loops at basement level in the rear wall of the
tower. The fort was completed in 1815 but it is uncertain if all the guns were mounted because seven years
later, in 1822, Inch Fort was described as 'a Sea
battery with traverse circles for six traversing plat-

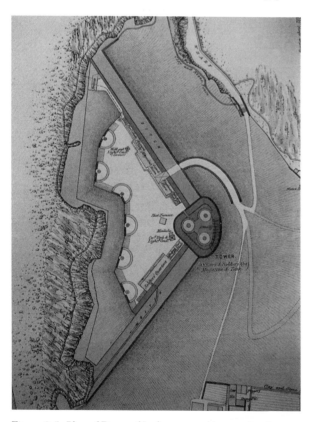

Figure 3.5: Plan of Down of Inch tower and battery dated
1863.The tower was built to the standard English east coast
design in 1814 and mounted three carronades for the defence of
the battery. The tower was demolished in 1897 when the fort
was rebuilt. (*TNA WO 78/4759*).

Figure 3.6: Knockalla (West Fort) from the air showing the remodelled Dunree (East) Fort in the background across the lough.

(Dermot Rainey)

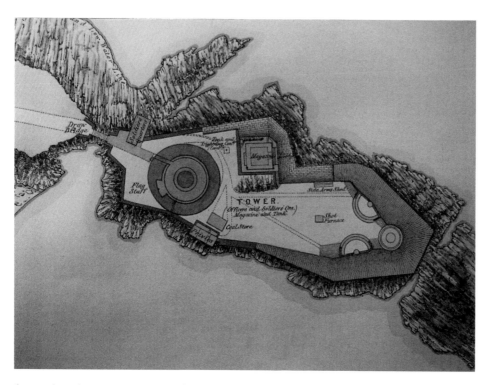

Figure 3.7: Plan of Macamish tower and battery dated 1863. (*TNA WO 78/4759*).

forms; has four guns 24 pounders mounted on platforms' and there is no mention of guns on the tower.[5]

In 1823 the garrisons of the forts and batteries along the shores of Lough Swilly were reduced to a bare minimum with only two or three Royal Artillery gunners and a few infantry soldiers allocated to each in order to maintain the guns and the general security of each fortification. In a report dated May 1823, for example, the garrison of the East Fort at Dunree comprised one NCO and two gunners of the Royal Artillery and eight infantrymen, while at the West Fort the garrison comprised two gunners and nine infantrymen. Although Inch Fort had accommodation for two officers, five NCOs and 80 soldiers in 1823 the garrison comprised a total of eight men: two gunners and six soldiers from a line battalion.[6]

Ten years later, in 1833, these garrisons were reduced still further as all the detachments of infantry had been withdrawn. At the battery on Macamish Point there were seven gunners with a further seven under the command of a Master Gunner at Dunree. All these gunners were drawn from a Royal Artillery company under the command of a captain that was stationed at Buncrana.

Master Gunners were responsible for the supervision of the ordnance, carriages, ammunition and stores in the forts or batteries at which they were stationed and by 1844 the only occupants of the East and West Forts were two Master Gunners. It would seem that they were the only occupants of the two forts as by that date the artillery company at Buncrana had been withdrawn. In 1851 a single gunner, from the Invalid Detachment, Royal Artillery at Woolwich, was stationed at Inch Fort which previously had been the responsibility of Bombardier Jackson RA who resided in the married quarter at Ned's Point Fort and was also responsible for the forts and batteries at Ned's Point, Rathmullen, and Macamish .

Between 1820 and 1847 there was no change in the armament of the Lough Swilly forts and batteries. but in that year the guns in the battery of East Fort, Dunree were replaced by modern guns of the same calibre and the two old 24-pounder SBML guns on the tower were removed and replaced by two 5 ½-in (140-mm) howitzers. At the West Fort at Knockalla the old French 42-pounder SBML guns remained in use but dwarf traversing platforms were installed in place of the older common traversing platforms.[7]

Despite a number of committees that sat to consider the defences of Ireland between 1850 and 1890 no move was made to modernise the defences of Lough Swilly. Indeed, in 1883 the West Fort at Knockalla was disarmed and the seven old French 42-pounder guns were made unserviceable and sold as scrap since the cost of removing them to Woolwich was more than they were worth. Two years later the newly formed Royal Artillery & Royal Engineers Works Committee, a War Office committee that had the role of advising the Defence Committee on coast fortifications in the United Kingdom, recommended that the defences of Lough Swilly should be dismantled except for Ned's Point Fort.

However, in 1889 there was a change of policy and the Admiralty and the War Office decided that Lough Swilly and Berehaven should be retained as fleet anchorages and harbours of refuge for merchant vessels in time of war. The Royal Artillery & Royal Engineers Works Committee paid another visit to Lough Swilly in 1889 and the committee's recommendation was that the defences of the lough should

be concentrated on the eastern shore since with modern breech-loading, rifled guns defences on the western shore were no longer necessary. The East Fort was to be re-armed with two 4.7-in (120-mm) QF guns, one of which was to be mounted on the 'tower' though the following year this was changed to a single 6-pounder QF gun on a cone mounting. In fact no modern guns were ever mounted on the tower of the fort at Dunree.

The batteries at Ned's Point and Inch Island were both remodelled to enable two 6-in BL guns on hydro-pneumatic mountings to be installed. In the case of the Inch battery this meant that the Martello tower was virtually demolished by being reduced in height to only a few feet above the ground. Both batteries were only in use for a period of about ten years. By 1912 a new battery of three 9.2-in (233-mm) BL guns was operational at Lenan Point at the entrance to the lough and a new battery of two 6-in (152-mm) BL guns had been built on Dunree Hill behind the old East Fort. These two batteries remained in use defending Lough Swilly until the end of the Second World War.

Today the East Fort at Dunree houses the Dunree

Figure 3.8: Macamish tower today. A large tower, similar to the Dublin 'Double' or two-gun towers, it is currently privately owned and used as a holiday home. (*Author's photograph*).

Military Museum, an unique coast artillery museum with the original guns of the battery still in place on the hill above the fort. On the other side of the lough the West Fort at Knockalla has passed through a number of owners without much having been done to restore it, though there are currently plans to construct a modern residence on the site of the old married quarter in the centre of the fort. However, the tower on Macamish Point has been a holiday home for many years and is in good condition. Inch Fort sadly is currently in a derelict condition and today only the lower level of the old tower remains incorporated into the new fort built in the 1890s.

Lough Foyle

Recommendations for the fortification of Lough Foyle had been made as early as 1796 since this sea lough led any invasion force straight to the city of Londonderry, the third largest city in Ireland at that time. However, no moves were made to provide defences for Londonderry until the arrival of the Committee of Engineers in the early months of 1806. Brigadier General Mann RE, the senior member of the committee, put forward a plan to build two forts to defend the lough, each comprising a tower for two guns and a battery of five guns. One fort was to be sited at Greencastle on the Donegal shore and the other opposite it on Magilligan Point in County Londonderry.

The proposals languished in the files of the Board of Ordnance, partly because of the dilatoriness of the Board in dealing with them and partly because of delay in finalising the plans for the forts. In April 1810 Colonel Fisher RE wrote to the Inspector General of Fortifications concerning the design of the tower at Greencastle. 'I have ventured to make an alteration in the Circular Tower proposed by the Committee, leaving out the projections and substituting a more simple profile'.[8] It is not clear what the 'projections' were, probably one or two *machicoulis*, but the final design adopted was for an oval rather than a circular tower.

There were also problems concerning the construction of the tower and battery at Magilligan Point because of the loose shifting sand. Indeed Magilligan Point is noted for the manner in which the sand dunes advance and retreat considerable distances over quite short periods of time as a result of tidal action. It was probably the realisation of the high costs that would be incurred in providing adequate foundations for both the tower and the battery that resulted in the cancellation of the plan to build a fort at Magilligan. So only the tower for two guns was eventually built on a foundation provided by a *grillage* of timber.[9]

Figure 3.9: The fort at Greencastle at the entrance to Lough Foyle The fort stands on the Donegal shore of the lough and this old postcard shows the tower and battery from the south east. (*Author's collection*).

Figure 3.10: The tower of Greencastle Fort showing the musketry loops at the base of the tower and the main gate of the fort. (*Author's photograph*).

The Lough Foyle works were authorised on 5th November 1811 but it would seem that once again Colonel Fisher and Captain Sir William Smith had difficulty in obtaining the requisite competitive tenders necessary to satisfy the Respective Officers in Dublin. Certainly Mr Edgar of Londonderry was considered the only competent local contractor when he was awarded the contracts for the Lough Swilly forts. Determined to obtain proper competitive tenders, the Respective Officers appear to have looked further afield for contractors who might be interested in tendering for the Lough Foyle contracts. They must have advertised in the Dublin newspapers for it was a Dublin contractor, Mr Edward Farrell, who submitted the lowest tender and obtained the contracts in 1812. As is so often the case, it would have been better had the Board of Ordnance rejected the lowest tender since Farrell was unable to complete the contract according to the terms of his tender. By March 1813 he was insolvent, his workers unpaid and his creditors, including a number of prominent citizens of Londonderry, also unpaid.

The problem stemmed from the fact that Farrell had been completely misled as to the cost of materials in Londonderry and the cost of transportation to the sites. Whether he was deliberately mis-advised or his informant was incompetent it is now impossible to judge. Suffice to say Farrell tendered basing his calculations on the cost of timber at £10 per ton when the actual cost was £12.10s and in his own words he 'sustained very heavy losses on almost every article of his contract too numerous to detail'.[10] He had already expended £4,000 more on the works at Greencastle than he had received and most of this sum was owed to nine Londonderry merchants.

In the opinion of Captain Carew, the Royal Engineers officer in charge of the actual construction work at Lough Swilly and Lough Foyle, the contract could only be completed on the same terms as those for the Lough Swilly works since no other contractor would be prepared to take over the contract. It would appear that his recommendation was accepted and the fort at Greencastle and the tower at Magilligan Point were finally completed in 1816-17.

The fort at Greencastle was designed as a tower for two guns and a battery for five 24-pounder SB guns. The battery was sited 35ft (10.75m) above the level of the lough, while the tower and the living quarters were a further 50ft (15.4m) above the battery. Two

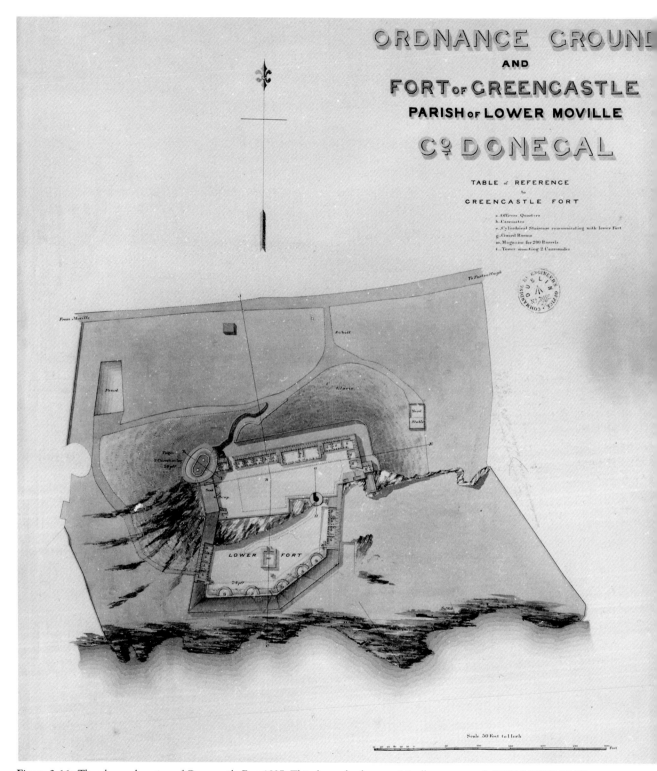

Figure 3.11: The plan and section of Greencastle Fort 1827. This shows the fort as originally constructed. *(TNA MPHH 1/641).*

Section on XY

Section and Elevation on DE

Section on ABC

Section on GH

24-pounder carronades were mounted on traversing platforms on the oval tower using individual locally-made pivots rather than unserviceable guns as was more usual in the English towers. No furnace was provided on the gun platform of the tower to heat shot as the guns mounted there were for the defence of the tower itself rather than for use against ships. However, rather surprisingly, there was no furnace provided for the battery, though it is possible a portable furnace was provided for use on the *terreplein* of the fort.

The tower was built of regular ashlar on a base of squared rubble masonry, the improved standard of workmanship of the upper section of the tower perhaps reflecting the change in Edward Farrell's fortunes. The tower stood 35ft (10.75m) high and was not shaped as a true oval but was more of a squashed cam shape in plan. It was also unusual in that the northern and southern ends of the parapet sloped down in a half circle at an angle of approximately 45 degrees for a distance of about 7ft (2.15m), a feature found in no other Martello tower and which may have been designed to cause enemy shot to ricochet off the tower rather than strike the parapet squarely.

On the north-east side overlooking the entrance to the fort and on the south-east side facing towards the lough there were two large windows and each was flanked by two apertures for ventilation. There was a stone staircase linking the first floor with the gun platform while the basement was entered through two trapdoors and down ladders. In the basement there was the magazine but there was also a firing gallery for riflemen using four loopholes almost level with the bottom of the tower. These loopholes and the window above defended the approach to the main gate of the fort which was situated adjacent to the tower.

The fort was very similar in area to the West Fort at Knockalla though less heavily armed. The design was obviously considered to be particularly successful as Colonel George Lewis RE used an almost identical design as an illustration for 'A Fort at the Entrance of a Harbour' in an article in 1844 on coast defence fortifications for the *Professional Papers of the Royal Engineers*.[11]

Figure 3.12: The gun platform of Greencastle tower. The photograph shows the pivots for the two 24-pounder carronades with which the tower was armed. (*Author's photograph*).

The second work designed to defend the entrance to Lough Foyle was constructed in the sandhills of Magilligan Point across the lough, immediately opposite Greencastle. This was a large circular two-gun tower, once again very similar in design to the large 'double' Dublin towers. The tower stood 200yds (185m) from the water's edge and, according to Major General Mann RE writing in 1810, was meant to co-operate with Greencastle Fort 'by producing a Drop Fire and also to scour its own shore'.[12]

Figure 3.13: Magilligan Martello tower on the County Londonderry shore of Lough Foyle. Together with Greencastle Fort on the opposite shore this tower defended the entrance to Lough Foyle. This photograph shows the tower in the 1950s with the WW2 Battery Observation Post still in place on the gun platform. (*Author's collection*).

The tower was built between 1812 and 1817 and is best described by quoting the Ordnance Survey Memoir for the parish of Magilligan, written in July 1835:

It is of circular form, 166 feet 10 inches [51.33m] in circumference measured above the basement, which is sunk 16 feet [4.9m] deep. The walls are 11 feet [3.3m] thick above and 13 feet [4m] below the basement of cut freestone from the quarries in Ballyharrigan in the parish of Bovevagh. It mounts one gun, which turns on a pivot and can be presented to any quarter. In the centre of the tower there is an excellent spring.[13]

The tower was 36ft (11.07m) high and was originally designed to mount two guns, though as we see from the Ordnance Survey Memoir quoted above it would seem that by 1835 it only mounted one. The tower had no central pillar but had supporting cross walls on each floor. The magazine was designed to hold two hundred barrels of gunpowder and the original copper door with bronze hinges may be seen in the tower today. Recessed into the parapet there was a shot furnace with two entrances and other recesses for made-up ammunition.

Figure 3.14: The magazine door of the Magilligan tower. The door is made of oak sheathed with copper and has bronze hinges. (*Author's photograph*).

Figure 3.15: The hot-shot furnace in the parapet of the Magilligan tower. This furnace is similar in design to those provided in some of the Dublin towers. (*Author's photograph*).

Figure 3.16: The gun platform of the Magilligan tower showing the position of the pivot for the two 24-pounder SB guns and the entrance to the staircase (left) and the shot furnace (centre & right). The racers for the guns were carried across each entrance on a removable wooden block. (*Author's photograph*).

The entrance was at first floor level but there are interesting hinges on each side of the entrance that seem to imply that at one stage the tower was entered by means of a small drawbridge possibly connecting with a set of steps which have now disappeared. Above the entrance there was a *machicoulis* and there was a window on each side of the tower but the side facing the lough was unbroken and, therefore, the

Figure 3.17: Magilligan Martello Tower today. The tower has been refurbished by the Heritage Department of the Northern Ireland Environment Agency. (*Author's photograph*).

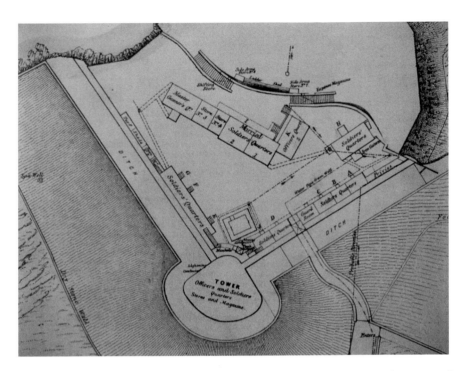

Figure 3.18: Mid 19th century plan of Knockalla (West) Fort (*Author's collection*).

strongest. Inside the tower, communication between all levels was by means of a staircase built into the rear wall.

In 1882 there were proposals to rearm both Greencastle Fort and the tower at Magilligan Point with more modern 64-pounder 71 cwt RML converted guns but although the *terreplein* of the battery at Greencastle Fort was remodelled to take heavier guns (which were never mounted) nothing was done to modernise the armament of the towers. Two years later, in 1884 the proposed defences of the lough were considered again when the Defence Committee decided on the rearming of Greencastle Fort with three 7-in (177-mm) RBL guns and the construction of a battery on Magilligan Point for three similar guns. The following year the Defence Committee authorised the transfer of three 7-in (177-mm) RBL guns on counterweight carriages from Fort Hubberstone in Milford Haven to Lough Foyle. These guns were destined to arm the new battery on Magilligan Point as the counterweight carriages were considered particularly suitable for positions on low-lying ground.[14] However, this decision to rearm the fort and tower was never implemented and in 1889 it was decided to dismantle both

Greencastle Fort and the tower at Magilligan Point and both were used for accommodation purposes with Magilligan Tower acting as a married quarter until well into the 1890s.

By the beginning of the First World War both Greencastle Fort and the Magilligan tower had been abandoned. The Magilligan tower was re-activated briefly during the Second World War when it was used as the battery observation post for an emergency coast defence battery of two 6-in (154-mm) BL naval guns manned by personnel of 381 Coast Battery RA and a concrete OP was built on the gun platform.

Today Greencastle Fort is privately owned, having been an hotel for a number of years. Sadly, the current owner obtained permission for a housing development to be built on the *terreplein* of the battery and this has resulted in the destruction of a large part of the lower area of the fort and the total destruction of the large magazine that was once capable of holding 400 barrels of gunpowder. The tower at Magilligan Point, on the other hand, has been refurbished by the Northern Ireland Environment Agency, the concrete OP has been removed and the tower is open to the public on application.

Chapter 4

THE GALWAY AND SHANNON TOWERS

Galway Bay

The west coast of Ireland offered many enticing landing places to an invader and Galway Bay, with the important town of Galway on its northern shore, was one of these. A landing in the area of Galway Town meant that Athlone, the main crossing place on the upper Shannon, was within relatively easy reach and from Athlone an invader could threaten Dublin itself. The strategic importance of Galway Bay had been noted as early as Cromwellian times when a star-shaped fort had been constructed on Rinmore Point and in 1702 a small fort had been built on Mutton Island, just off Galway harbour. In 1740 a return of ordnance showed that there were 93

'pieces of cannon' and one brass mortar defending Galway but that almost all were dismounted and unserviceable except for five, and the carriages of four of these were broken and rotten.[1]

By 1747 the fortifications were reported as being entirely out of repair and in a ruinous condition and it was recommended that the battery on Mutton Island should be re-erected but nothing was done and in 1779 the Abbey Gate was pulled down. In 1792 another observer commented that 'for more than half a century the fortifications had been going fast to decay… and the remainder of these mouldering bulwarks were falling to the ground'.[2] In 1803, appreciating the vulnerability of Galway Town to an

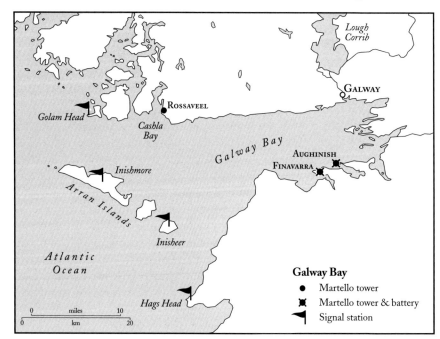

Figure 4.1: Galway Bay towers and signal stations. (*Martin Brown*)

Figure 4.2: Aughinish tower on Aughinish Island on the southern shore of Galway Bay. The tower was built to the standard English east coast design and mounted one 'heavy' and two 'short' guns. (*Author's photograph*).

enemy attack, General Lord Cathcart instructed Brigadier General Fisher RE to construct three Martello towers for the defence of the town and bay. One of the proposed towers was to have been built on Mutton Island to defend the entrance to Galway harbour with another at Newhaven (also known as New Harbour), a bay some miles west of Oranmore. The third tower was to defend a landing place on the southern shore of Galway Bay at Finavarra in County Clare. These towers were not built at this time and the Finavarra tower was the only one of the three Galway towers included in Brigadier General Fisher's list of towers under construction or planned that was subsequently to be built but not until ten years later.

In April 1804, with the threat from Napoleon at its height, eight 24-pounder guns 'for the defence of the Anchoring-ground and Harbour of Galway' were listed with guns for the defence of the Shannon at Athlone. These may well have been intended for Mutton and Hare Island but there is no indication that batteries on these two islands were ever built.[3]

Brigadier General Fisher's list was followed in 1804 by a report from General Lord Cathcart to HRH The Duke of York in which he recommended that Galway Town should be refortified with the construction of

towers on Taylor's Hill, Mutton Island and Rinmore Point together with seven redoubts surrounding the town and towers to be built at Cashla Bay on the north shore of the bay and at Finavarra and Oranmore on the south shore. Nothing came of this plan to refortify Galway Town or construct the towers but in 1810 another Committee of Engineers reviewed the defences of Ireland and this time paid particular attention to Galway Bay. Black Head and the Burren were unfavourable stretches of country for an army to move across so the committee identified Finavarra, on the eastern shore of Ballyvaughan Bay, and the adjoining Aughinish Island as possible sites for an enemy landing. The committee recommended that two large Martello towers should be built to defend the area and the towers were built to the English East coast design.[4]

These towers were cam-shaped and mounted one heavy 'long' gun, a 24-pounder SBML gun, and two 5½-in howitzers on the gun platform and each tower had an adjacent battery although today the batteries have disappeared. The guns on the towers may have originally been mounted on wooden traversing platforms but later in the century the wooden platform for the heavy gun was replaced with an iron one. The

Figure 4.3: The central pillar supporting the bomb-proof gun platform of Aughinish tower. (*Author's photograph*).

height of each tower was 33ft (10.15m) and the diameter 55ft (16.9m) and they were constructed of granite ashlar. The wall of the tower had a batter and there were four windows with a door at first floor level as in other Martello towers. The interior accommodation of the towers was standard with the officer and other ranks accommodated on the first floor which was divided into two rooms each with a fireplace. The ground floor or basement consisted of the magazine and stores and, unusually, in both towers a plan of 1861 showed that the ground floor was divided into 'magazine, wine cellar and store'![5] The cost of the construction of the two towers came to a total of £8,026.14s.3d.[6]

A third Martello tower was built to defend a small bay, Cashla Bay, near Rossaveel about 20 miles (32 km) due west of Galway Town. Cashla Bay, a long narrow inlet with sandy beaches at the head of the bay and on either side, was one of the locations to be defended originally identified by Lord Cathcart. Although identified by Lord Cathcart and the Committee of Engineers as a possible landing place for French forces Cashla Bay was considered to be of less importance than either Finavarra or Aughinish and so a smaller tower was considered adequate for its defence. Nevertheless, it is difficult to see what value

Figure 4.4: Finavarra tower, situated some three miles west of Aughinish tower, was built to the same design. (*Author's photograph*).

there was in siting a single tower without a supporting battery in a remote location such as Rossaveel. Any enemy force landing there would be faced with the extensive barrier formed by Lough Corrib and would be forced to attack Galway Town or make a long detour north via Cong before reaching easier terrain on the march to the Shannon.

The tower was sited on the eastern shore of the bay at its narrowest point and once again the decision was taken to use an English-pattern tower, but this time it was the smaller south coast design that was used. The tower was elliptical in plan and was armed with a single 24-pounder SBML long gun and one 8-in (203mm) calibre brass howitzer. Although generally similar in design to the Kent and Sussex towers the Cashla Bay tower differed in two important aspects. The batter to the wall stopped about 6ft (1.8m) below the top of the parapet and internally there was no central pillar supporting the gun platform. Like the other Galway Bay towers the tower at Cashla Bay was built of granite ashlar and had a height of 33ft (10.15m) but its diameter was considerably smaller at 45ft (13.85m). In 1816 a report stated that this tower could accommodate a garrison of one officer and 28 men, a large number considering that there was no battery to be manned.[7]

Figure 4.5: The doorway of Finavarra tower. The photograph clearly shows the chute between the bars of which the entrance ladder could be drawn up. (*Author's photograph*).

Figure 4.6: The tower at Cashla Bay, west of Galway Town. This tower is very similar in design to the English south coast towers except that the batter of the wall ceases about six feet (1.85 m) from the top of the parapet. (*Author's photograph*).

The cost of the construction of the tower came to £3,115.9s.6d.[8]

In 1823 the tower at Cashla Bay was taken over by the Preventative Water Guard, a forerunner of the Coastguard, and in 1835 the Master General of the Ordnance in London ordered that all batteries in Ireland not protecting merchant shipping should be dismantled. The view of the CRE in Dublin was that as it cost so little annually to maintain the towers they should be retained and the Master General accepted his view. However, as the towers at Aughinish and Finavarra were particularly damp and not suited to permanent accommodation it was agreed that these two towers should be shut up but the garrison of four gunners from the Invalid Battalion RA retained. These gunners and their families were accommodated in the villages closest to the two towers.

Thirty five years later in its 'General Report upon the Defence of Commercial Harbours of the United Kingdom' the Committee on Home Defence reviewed the defences of Galway. The committee reported that the towers at Auginish, Finavarra and Rossaveel were too distant to be of any defence to the port of Galway and there was no proposal to rearm the towers.[9] In 1859 the garrison of the Galway Bay towers was a Master Gunner and four Invalid gunners but the three towers were abandoned in 1863 and the Aughinish and Finavarra towers were let commercially in 1869 and 1870 respectively. Although the towers had been abandoned their heavy guns remained on the gun platforms. All the equipment including the 5½-in howitzers was removed but it was not possible, or perhaps economic, to remove the 24-pounder SBML guns each weighing 50cwt (1.27 tonnes) and so these old guns were left on top of the towers together with their iron traversing platforms until quite recently.

Today all three Martello towers in Galway Bay can still be seen and visited. Their continued existence is probably due to the fact that they are situated in such isolated locations and although stripped of most of their woodwork the stone of the towers remained in very reasonable condition. This enabled the tower at Aughinish to enjoy a new lease of life as it has now been converted into a private residence. The Finavarra tower is now the responsibility of the Irish State since it has been bequeathed to the State for the benefit of the nation by its late owner. Today a plaque on the site has the following inscription:

> This property including the Martello Tower and Appurtenances was bequeathed to the State for the benefit of the Nation by Mrs Maureen Emerson who died on the 4th day of November 1999.

Upper Shannon

The two main crossings over the upper reaches of the River Shannon are at Athlone and at Shannonbridge 12 miles (19km) downstream from Athlone. In 1803 a medieval castle and a line of redoubts defended the bridge at Athlone while Shannonbridge was defended by a number of earthen batteries erected as field works. However, in 1810 a Committee of Engineers considered the defences of Athlone and the River Shannon and recommended extending the line of redoubts and constructing two three-gun towers each with a supporting battery on two areas of high ground east of the river. One tower was to be built on Mourne's Hill to the north of Athlone and the other on Anchor's Bower south east of the town. As the threat from Napoleon diminished and with it the threat of invasion so the construction of these towers assumed a lower priority in the scheme of things. The building of the tower on Anchor's Bower was delayed and finally cancelled because of doubts as to there being sufficient ground on the hill for the construction of a large tower and the tower proposed for Mourne's Hill became a victim of financial cuts.

Apart from the bridges at Athlone and Shannonbridge there were other crossings over the Shannon. There was another bridge, similar to the one at Shannonbridge, at Banagher in County Offaly (at that time King's County) and two fords; one at Keelogue, four miles (6.4kms) downstream from Banagher, and the other at Meelick, a short distance below Keelogue.

The bridge at Banagher was considered to be as important as that at Shannonbridge and instructions were issued in late 1803 that steps should be taken to provide defences to protect the bridge. A canal ran along the west bank of the river and parallel to it

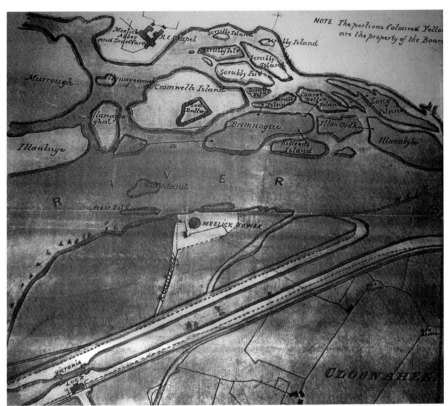

Figure 4.7: Sketch map showing the tower at Meelick in relation to Meelick Abbey and the sod battery on Cromwell's Island. 1853. (*TNA WO 44/719*)

Figure 4.8: The tower at Banagher built to the standard English south coast design and mounting a single heavy gun. This is one of the few Martello towers built to defend an inland site. (*Author's photograph*).

forming an additional line of defence and there was an old seventeenth century fortification, Cromwell's Castle, standing between the canal and the river. The steps taken to improve the defences of the crossing did not go as far as building a sophisticated *tete de pont* as at Shannonbridge, but, instead the old castle was improved and strengthened enabling it to mount two 12-pounder SBML guns. In addition, a battery of three 12-pounder SBML guns was installed in the barrack yard of the small infantry barracks at the eastern end of the bridge and another battery for three 18-pounder SBML guns constructed as a 'Field Work' in the marshy ground on the left of the bridge. This battery was subsequently improved and named Fort Eliza.

The committee also recommended a further strengthening of the Banagher defences by the construction of a Martello tower to be sited west of the canal and named Fanesker Tower. Here again the design used was that of the English south coast towers and the tower was elliptical in plan and the north west side of the wall was thicker than the rest of the wall as that was the direction any attack could be

expected to come from. The doorway was at first floor level and on the south east side of the tower facing the river. The tower was built of dressed stone, had two windows but, unlike the English tower on which it was modelled there was no central pillar supporting the bomb-proof gun platform and, instead, support was provided by an internal brick dome. The armament of the tower was a single 24-pounder heavy SBML gun on a traversing platform. As in the English towers the magazine was in the basement but there was no cistern for storing fresh water and, instead, water was provided by means of a well. The cost of the tower was estimated at £3,064 16s. 8d.

At Keelogue the decision was taken to defend the ford by means of a seven-gun battery secured at the gorge by a defensible guardhouse rather than a Martello tower but at the lesser ford at Meelick a three-gun Martello tower, similar in design to the English east coast towers, was deemed adequate protection. The tower was sited on Collinrea Island opposite an existing five-gun sod battery on Cromwell's Island which it was to replace. Because the tower at Meelick was larger than the one at

Figure 4.9: Cromwell's Castle (left) and the Martello tower (right) defending the bridge over the River Shannon at Banagher. A watercolour painted by Captain Sir William Smith, Assistant Engineer at Lough Swilly, in 1814. Cromwell's Castle was a 17th century fortification that had its gun platform strengthened in 1806. (*The Board of Trinity College, Dublin*)

Figure 4.10: Meelick tower, hidden behind a large spread of ivy, was built to defend a ford across the River Shannon. This was an English east coast pattern tower, a design probably selected because, unlike at Banagher, this was the only fortification defending this important crossing and there was no other battery. (*Author's photograph*).

Banagher the cost of construction was considerably more at £3,948 14s. 9¾d.

Like the large English towers the Meelick tower was cam-shaped and identical with the towers at Aughinish and Finavarra on the shores of Galway Bay. The tower was built of dressed stone with a magazine and storeroom in the basement; living accommodation on the first floor; and the armament on the trefoil-shaped gun platform comprised one 24-pounder heavy SBML gun and two 5½-in howitzers on traversing platforms. The entrance was at first-floor level where there were two windows, one at each side of the tower, and two staircases built into the thickness of the wall leading up to the gun platform. Unlike the Fanesker Tower at Banagher the Meelick tower had a central pillar supporting the gun platform. Built into the inner wall of the parapet there were a number of arched recesses for the storage of ready-to-use cartridges, shot and shells for the gun and the howitzers mounted on the tower.

These two towers were among a small number of Martello towers not sited to defend a section of coastline. Their role was to defend crossings over the Shannon and they were completed by 1816 just after the war with Napoleon had ended! Although both towers were maintained for a number of years, by 1859 it was recognised that they were obsolete and no attempt was made to re-arm them. The advent of the railways in Ireland had also reduced the strategic importance of Athlone other than for internal security reasons and by 1884 it had ceased to be a key point in the defence of Ireland. Both towers had remained armed as late as 1844 but in 1863 the battery at Keelogue and the towers had been disarmed and were disposed of shortly after that date. Today the Fanesker Tower is privately owned and in good condition but the tower at Meelick, which had been transferred to the Public Works Board in 1856, stands derelict in the middle of a field, covered in ivy and abandoned to the elements.

Chapter 5

THE WEXFORD AND LOUTH TOWERS

Wexford

The Wexford towers built at Fort Point near Rosslare and Baginbun Point near Fethard were two of the earliest Martello towers to be built in Ireland, their construction being started not long after the towers on Bere Island. As early as 1803 there had been a proposal from Lord Hardwicke, the Lord Lieutenant, for signal stations to be established around the coast of Ireland. As Ireland was in an unsettled state at that time the Admiralty suggested to the Lord Lieutenant that 'Corsican towers' or Martello towers should be built to defend the signal stations but this suggestion was dismissed by Hardwicke who believed that a less expensive form of tower would suffice except in situ-

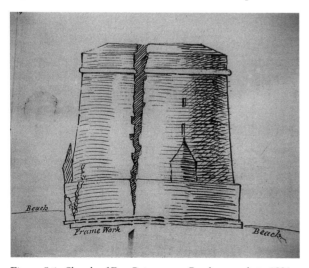

Figure 5.1: Sketch of Fort Point tower, Rosslare, made in 1821 showing the damage that was caused by sea erosion which subsequently resulted in the demolition of the tower. This sketch, though very rough, is the only depiction of this tower that the author has been able to discover. *(TNA WO 44/108)*.

ations where they might be required for defence against an enemy landing. As a result only two Martello towers were built for use as signal towers and these were the Rosslare and Baginbun Point towers. The tower at Rosslare was built on Fort Point to defend the entrance to the harbour while the Baginbun tower was built on Baginbun Head near Fethard to defend a nearby anchorage. Both towers were originally built as 'Field Works' but subsequently responsibility for their maintenance was taken on by the Board of Ordnance.

The Fort Point tower at Rosslare had a somewhat chequered start to its construction because of the uncertainty as to whether a Martello tower should be built rather than a defensible signal tower. In September 1804 it was reported that at the Fort Point 'a Tower begun but stopped by order – uncertain whether any contract has been entered into for Building a Martello Tower which was proposed should answer for a Signal Tower'.[1] Obviously this was eventually settled and the two towers were complete by February 1806 having been built by the same contractor, according to Sir Arthur Wellesley, later the Duke of Wellington, who reported on the towers when touring the defences of the south and south-west of Ireland when he was Chief Secretary in July 1806.[2]

Both towers were similar in design to the Dublin towers though the Baginbun tower was unique amongst the Irish towers in having four *machicoulis* at parapet level, one in each quadrant of the tower wall. This may well have been because the Baginbun tower stood on its own unsupported by a battery unlike the Fort Point tower which was sited close to Rosslare

Figure 5.2: Baginbun tower. Now converted into a holiday home the tower stands in good condition. The photograph shows three of the four *machicoulis*. (*Author's photograph*).

Fort. The wall of each tower was built with a batter using granite ashlar and had a string course at the base of the parapet. The dimensions of these towers were similar to those of the Dublin towers but the construction costs were considerably higher at £9,000 for the two which probably reflected an increased cost for the Baginbun tower which was in an isolated location. Both towers were complete by February 1806.

The Baginbun tower did not have a central pillar but did have the usual first floor level entrance and two slanting ventilation shafts one on each side of the entrance. There was also an ammunition shaft leading up to the gun platform from the entrance passage as in a number of the Dublin towers and in towers built by the British on the island of Minorca in the Mediterranean. A staircase in the wall led from the first floor to the gun platform and one of the *machicoulis* was entered from the stairwell. It is assumed that the tower on Fort Point at Rosslare was built with similar features but with only one *machicoulis* and that over the entrance.

The towers were each armed initially with a single 24-pounder carronade, a rather inadequate armament for anything but defence against an attack by infantry and, certainly, quite useless for defence of Rosslare Harbour. Certainly Wellesley agreed for he noted

that both towers 'had a material fault' in only having a carronade as armament and recommended that it should be replaced by an 18-pounder gun.[3] The Chief Secretary's suggestion was eventually taken up and some years later the carronade on each tower was removed and replaced with a 12-pounder gun.

Wellesley also reported on an unusual feature of the Fort Point tower concerning its water supply. The usual method of providing water for Martello towers was by means of a cistern in the basement filled manually from an external source or by means of a rainwater drainage system from the gun platform. In the case of the Rosslare tower Wellesley reported that 'water is found by digging within the Tower into the land which although within 50 yards [46m] of the sea is quite good'[4]

The Rosslare tower appears to have had a relatively short life as it was soon in danger of erosion by the sea. At the conclusion of the war in 1815 the tower was occupied by boatmen of the Revenue Service but by 1819 sea erosion had caused a huge split in the wall of the tower which made the tower uninhabitable. In March 1819 it was dismantled and surrendered to the Commissioners for the Improvement of the Town and Harbour of Wexford until it split in two in 1821 and was finally demolished, much against the wishes of the Commissioners of Wexford Harbour because the tower was used as a navigation aid by ships entering the harbour.

For some years after the end of the war with Napoleon Baginbun tower was occupied by a small detachment of Invalid (Pensioner) gunners from the Invalid Battalion RA and by 1860 the Army had vacated the tower and no mention of it appears in the reports after 1850. The tower was purchased in 1947 from a local priest and converted into a private residence which it remains today.

Two other towers were built in County Wexford, both at Duncannon Fort overlooking the entrance to Waterford Harbour. Duncannon Fort was the main fortification defending the entrance to Waterford Harbour. It was an old fort dating from the mid-

Figure 5.3: Duncannon No.1 tower. This tower and its companion, No.2 tower, was built to the standard English south coast design and sited to protect the high ground overlooking the rear of Fort Duncannon. *(Author's photograph).*

seventeenth century and by 1804 it was armed with 28 heavy guns. However, it suffered from the disadvantage that so many fortifications, particularly coastal fortifications, suffered from, that of being dominated by higher ground to its rear. Colonel Twiss had commented on this when he inspected the Irish defences in 1803 and three years later, in 1806, a Committee of Engineers headed by Brigadier General Gother Mann also reviewed the defences and recommended the construction of three towers at Duncannon. Two of these towers were to secure the high ground to the rear of the fort and the third, somewhat unusually, was to defend the entrance to the fort.

Construction of the two towers for the defence of the high ground commenced in 1812 and the towers were built half a mile (812m) apart. By this stage in the war it would appear that the Board of Ordnance in London was encouraging the Commanding Royal Engineer in Dublin to standardise the design of the Martello towers in Ireland by using the designs for the towers built in England. In the case of the Duncannon towers which were each to mount one heavy gun Brigadier General Fisher adopted the English south-coast design for a tower elliptical in plan similar to those built at Cashla Bay in County Galway and at Banagher in County Offaly.

Both towers were built of granite ashlar and had a height of 32 feet (10m) with the thickest portion of the wall nine feet (3m) thick. There was a bomb-proof roof supporting the gun platform but no central pillar and, unlike the Dublin and Bere Island towers, no string course at the base of the parapet and no *machicoulis*. The first floor was divided into two rooms each with a window and a fireplace. Entrance to the tower was, as usual, at first floor level and by means of a ladder. There was a single stone staircase built into the wall and the basement was divided into a storeroom and a magazine. As was the case with the tower on Fort Point at Rosslare water was provided by means of a well rather than a cistern which was more usual in the majority of Martello towers.

Interestingly, there seems to have been some doubt in the mind of the engineer in charge of the building of the towers as to their role. The towers were built

Figure 5.4:
Duncannon No.2
tower. This tower has
now been converted
into a private
residence. *(Author's
photograph)*.

with the thickest section of the wall facing the sea and with the door on the landward side, yet the towers were built with the express role of defending Duncannon Fort from a land attack and not an attack from the sea!

The third tower for the defence of the entrance to the fort was to have been of the same design as the towers on the high ground to the rear of the fort. However, work on this tower was never commenced and there was considerable correspondence between Colonel Fyers and the Inspector General of Fortifications, General Morse, on the subject. There was also debate on the matter of the best form of flank protection for the South Front of the fort and in August 1812 a casemated battery was proposed 'about 50ft (15.3m) below the level of the Gun in the (proposed) Tower' as being 'as complete a Flank for the South Front as any work can have'.[5] As a result the third tower was cancelled in the same month and a *place d'armes* on the glacis was substituted for it.

The towers were in use for only a comparatively short period of time. Lewis in his *Topographical Dictionary of Ireland* published in 1837 describes the two towers as being 'dismantled'. It seems that one of the towers was garrisoned briefly during the 'Fenian Crisis' of the 1860s as in 1868 a group of 20 'Fenians' was reported as attempting to capture the tower. The 'Fenians' opened fire on the tower one night in January 1868 but they were quickly repulsed by the garrison of the fort. Tower No.1 was briefly used by the Irish Army during the Second World War, or 'Emergency' as it was known in Eire, and both towers are now privately owned.

Louth

Only one tower was built to the north of the Dublin towers and that was at Drogheda in County Louth. This tower was proposed in September 1807 though it was not a true Martello tower since there was no gun platform as such and the tower was primarily a guardhouse for a battery. Known as Richmond Fort the tower and battery were sited on the Millmount, a prominent hill standing 140ft (43m) overlooking the town and the bridge over the River Boyne. However, the role of the tower was actually stated as being a signal tower as when the tower was first proposed it 'would as a signal post be useful in communicating with the different Yeomanry Corps in the neighbourhood the alarm posts of three or four of them being within sight of it'. It was proposed that the battery should comprise two 12-pounder guns.[6]

The proposal was to build a tower of two storeys to accommodate about 25 or 30 men, with a small apartment for an officer and a magazine and a storeroom together with a cistern in the lower storey. The lack of a gun platform was explained by Colonel Fisher in a letter to the Inspector General of Fortifications as follows: 'As the situation is high and commanding there seems to be no necessity for a parapet on top of the guardhouse. I have therefore proposed a sturdy boarded roof covered with slates, which will not only render the building more comfortable, but will do away with the objection of its being liable to be scaled or taken by surprise in the night – the projecting courses, or machicoulis, will protect the

entrance and see pretty near the foot of the Guardhouse.'[7] Unusually, this was the only tower built on the east coast of Ireland that originated from the Board of Ordnance, all the others starting as 'Field Works' and it was completed in March 1809 by the contractor Mr George Chace under the direction of Captain George Wright, RE. As so often happened in Ireland with the construction of fortifications the tower was not completed without a dispute between the contractor and the Royal Engineer officer supervising the construction of the tower. Captain Wright reported to the commanding Royal Engineer in Dublin that the 'Works [were] by no means well or substantially executed, are deficient in grouting, that the measurements are erroneous and the prices not correct'.[8] There followed a long-drawn out inquiry which resulted in the contract being withdrawn from the contractor.

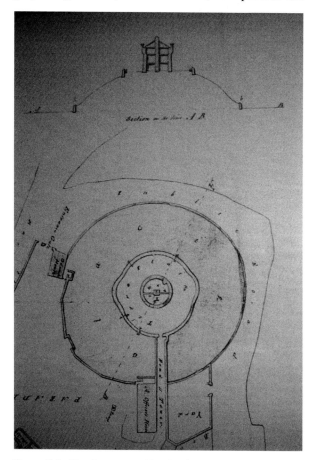

Figure 5.5: Plan & section of Fort Richmond tower and battery. Built on the Millmount overlooking Drogheda the tower had a role as a signal tower and keep of last resort. *(TNA WO 44/581).*

Figure 5.6: Richmond Fort after its capture by Irish government forces during the Irish Civil War in 1922. *(Author's collection).*

Figure 5.7: Fort Richmond tower which has recently been restored. It did not have a gun platform on top but supported a battery of two 9-pounder SB guns at its base. (*Author's photograph*).

The tower was 35ft (10.7m) in height with a diameter of 32ft (9.2m) and, as the tower was essentially a musketry tower, there was a line of large musket loops at first-floor level and a further line of smaller ones in the wall of the floor above, which partially projected out from the wall beneath supported on projecting courses. As there was no bombproof roof or gun platform there was no requirement for a central supporting pillar. Communication between the floors of the tower was by means of a stone staircase partially set into the wall while above the doorway there was an opening in the course that acted as a *machicoulis*. Although the original intention was to mount two 12-pounder guns in the battery at the base of the tower, in the end two, lighter, 9-pounder guns were mounted there.

The guns were removed in 1863 but the British Army continued to occupy the tower and barracks which were used as the headquarters for the Louth (Rifles) Militia, 6th Battalion the Royal Irish Rifles, until 1908 when the battalion was disbanded as a result of the Haldane reforms. The tower subsequently was occupied by rebel forces during the Irish Civil War in 1922 and was retaken by Irish government forces under a Captain Stapleton after the tower had been bombarded by the government forces using an 18-pounder QF field gun in August 1922. As a result of the bombardment the tower was badly damaged but recently the damage has been repaired and the tower and barracks converted into an excellent museum complex.

Chapter 6

THE CORK TOWERS

Cork, in the late eighteenth and early nineteenth-century the city in Ireland second only to Dublin, lies at the head of a large natural harbour, the best anchorage of its size in Ireland. At this period Cork was an important commercial centre and base for the Royal Navy, particularly during the French Revolutionary war and the Napoleonic war. In 1793 the defences of this important harbour comprised two forts, Fort Carlisle and Fort Camden defending the entrance to the harbour; an old fort on Spike Island, a large island at the head of the harbour; and a small battery at Cobh, covering the channel between Spike Island and the mainland.

In his report of January 1803 Colonel Twiss RE recommended that the Cork Harbour defences should be improved by building a new large, pentagonal bastioned fortress on Spike Island; the retention of Fort Carlisle on the eastern headland at the entrance to the harbour and also the battery at Cobh. Interestingly, Twiss recommended that Fort Camden should be demolished. General Cornwallis, the Commander-in-Chief of the army in Ireland supported the proposal for a new fortress on Spike Island and work on the new Fort Westmoreland commenced in June 1804.

In 1805 General Lord Cathcart, the new commander of the forces in Ireland, reviewed the defences of Cork Harbour and ordered work to be

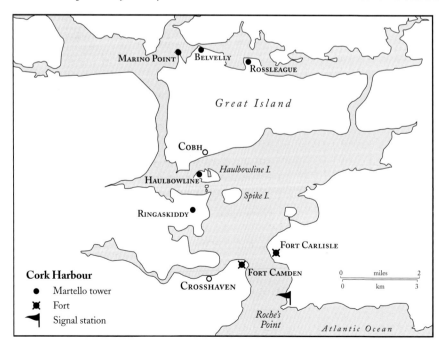

Figure 6.1: Cork Harbour – Martello towers, forts and signal stations. (*Martin Brown*)

Figure 6.2: The tower on Ringaskiddy Hill on the western shore of Cork Harbour. This was the largest of the Cork Martello towers and which, together with the other Cork towers and unlike other British towers, had a wall without a batter. (*Author's photograph*).

carried out to improve Forts Camden and Carlisle and the battery at Cobh. Work continued on Fort Westmoreland on Spike Island and a new battery was constructed at Roche's Tower on Roche's Point, south of Fort Carlisle at the entrance to the harbour. At the same time the Chief Secretary in Ireland, William Wellesley Pole, suggested the move of the naval store depot from Kinsale to Haulbowline Island in Cork Harbour.

Two years previously the Board of Ordnance took the decision to remove the Cork fortifications from the control of the Commanding Royal Engineer in Dublin and established it as a separate district with its own Commanding Royal Engineer, Lieutenant Colonel Sir Charles Holloway RE, reporting directly to the Inspector General of Fortifications in London. This decision appears to have been taken because of the importance of Cork and the number of fortifications under construction both there and in Bantry Bay.

In January 1806 the Committee of Engineers consisting of Brigadier General Gother Mann and Lieutenant Colonel Robert D'Arcy RE reviewed the Irish defences and their recommendations for the defence of Cork Harbour included the completion of

Fort Westmoreland and the retention of Fort Camden. In addition, the Mann committee proposed that five Martello towers should be built for the defence of the harbour, one on Haulbowline Island, one on Ringaskiddy Hill to secure high ground on the western shore of the harbour that overlooked Spike Island and three towers on Great Island (sometimes confusingly referred to as Cove Island in Board of Ordnance papers of the time) to guard the fords and a bridge between the island and the mainland. These latter towers were to be sited at Marino Point and Belvelly on the north western shore of Great Island and at Rossleague a mile and a quarter (2 kms) to the east of Belvelly.

Although the Mann committee reported on the defences of Ireland in January 1806 it was not until 1811 that deteriorating relations with the United States of America and another, albeit abortive, French invasion scare concentrated the minds of the officers of the Board of Ordnance in London and the decision was taken to build the towers. All five towers were to be large towers with the cost of the three on Great Island being estimated in 1811 at £16,570. 8s.9d. and the towers on Ringaskiddy Hill and Haulbowline Island at £3,808.14s.1d. and £3,092.13s.2d. respectively.[1]

The tower on Ringaskiddy Hill was to be 'a tower of the largest dimensions with ditch and glacis. For two 24 pounders to be sunk as low as possible consistent with command of the ground around it'.[2] On Haulbowline Island 'a tower for one gun may be sufficient here 'while on Great (Cove) Island 'the tower for two guns or one long gun and one short one or one carronade. The diameter of the tower to be proportional accordingly. No ditch or counterscarp'.[3]

The three towers on Great(Cove) Island were to defend Belvelly (Belleville) Bridge and the fords at Manning Point and Rossleague. In 1808 Lieutenant Colonel Fenwick, the Commanding Royal Engineer in Cork, who had replaced Sir Charles Holloway, originally considered that the tower of the old Belvelly Castle 'might be filled up to serve as one of the Towers proposed'.[4] This idea was rejected but it is interesting to note that a loophole for a machine gun was inserted into the wall of the tower of the castle overlooking the approach to the bridge in 1940 during the 'Emergency'.

All the towers were constructed of limestone ashlar with brick-lined interiors and the Rossleague and Haulbowline towers were slightly oval in plan while the others were circular. All the towers stood approximately 40ft (12.3m) high but varied in diameter. The largest was Ringaskiddy with an overall diameter of 51ft (15.7m) while the others were somewhat smaller, with diameters around 45-48ft (13.8-14.75m). The Ringaskiddy Hill tower was the only tower with a ditch and glacis, the ditch being 10ft (3m) deep and 18ft (5.5m) wide.

Unlike the other Irish towers, except the rebuilt tower on Garinish Island in Glengarriff Harbour near Bantry, the Cork towers had no batter to the external wall. This was because Lieutenant Colonel Fenwick believed that 'the walls [of buildings] in this country [Ireland] should be made perpendicular and not sloping, there is no advantage that I know of in the latter mode, and it certainly may expose them more to the effect of driving rain'.[5]

The interior of the towers followed a standard pattern with four compartments, including the magazine, on the ground (basement) floor, and two accommodation rooms on the first floor. Each room had a window and a fireplace and the entrance to the tower was at this level. The door of the Ringaskiddy tower

Figure 6.3: Ringaskiddy tower. The photograph shows a section of the deep ditch that still surrounds the tower together with a section of the masonry counterscarp. (Author's photograph).

Figure 6.4: The Belvelly tower defending the Belvelly bridge linking Great Cove Island with the mainland. A photograph taken in 1903. (*Author's collection*).

was on the side of the tower facing the sea, indicating that its role was to defend the approach from the land side and access was by means of a drawbridge across the ditch. In the other Cork towers access was by way of the usual ladder that could be withdrawn into the tower. The ground floor door in Rossleague tower which can be seen today is a later addition. In each of the five towers the gun platform was supported by a bomb-proof arch rather than a central pillar. Communication between the floors within the towers was by means of a stone staircase partially built into the wall of the tower. The magazine in the base-

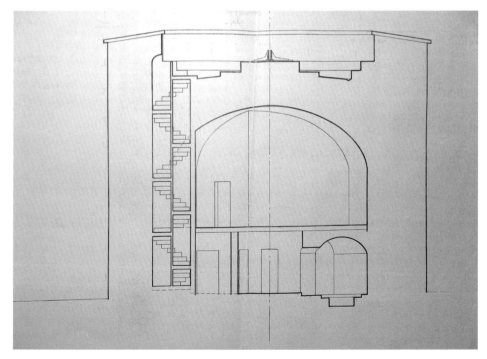

Figure 6.5: Section of Rossleague Tower, Great Island. (*Paul Kerrigan*)

Figure 6.6: The tower on Haulbowline Island in Cork Harbour. The tower has been refurbished for use by the Irish Naval Service as a museum but is now closed. *(Author's photograph)*

ment, or ground floor, had a capacity of 100 barrels of gunpowder.

All the towers except the tower on Haulbowline Island were designed to mount two guns, with Ringaskiddy mounting two 'long' 24-pounders and the others one 24 pounder 'long' gun and a second 24 pounder 'short' gun or carronade each on a traversing platform but it would seem that only the 'long' gun was ever mounted on each tower. On many Martello towers the traversing platforms rotated on a pivot constructed from an unserviceable gun mounted barrel upwards in the floor of the gun platform with a spike projecting from the muzzle. However when the Cork towers were being constructed no unserviceable guns were available in Ireland so locally-designed and

made cast-iron pivots had to be provided. Each pivot took the form of vertical pin supported on six legs in the shape of a star and were similar to the pivots on Greencastle Tower on the shores of Lough Foyle and on other towers built in Ireland at this period.

The move of the naval store depot from Kinsale to Haulbowline Island in Cork Harbour forced the Board of Ordnance to consider what part of the island they felt should be retained for defence purposes. A report on the subject in 1805 stated: 'It appears that a part of it [Haulbowline Island] should be retained by the Ordnance for a tower, or some other tenable work as it is situated nearly in front of a small navigable channel that runs round the South West side of Spike Island and would also have a reverse fire on the West and North side of that island; besides it is in some degree on the flank of any batteries that might be erected on the distant height of Ringaskiddy; it also looks down the narrow part of the principal channel leading to Cork, and all ships bound thither must pass close to the island'.[6]

The decision was taken to divide the island in half, one part administered by the Board of Ordnance and the other by the Board of Admiralty. It is perhaps a reflection of the state of relations between the Ordnance and the Admiralty that a wall was built bisecting the island into two halves with a single gate providing access between each half! The original idea for a 'tenable work' was that it should be a quadrangular tower or defensible guardhouse similar to those built on the Shannon and the shores of Lough Swilly (which will be described in Chapter 7) but this plan was later changed to a circular Martello tower of the same design and dimensions as the other Cork towers.

The contracts for the construction of the towers were awarded to two local contractors, Messrs Richard Cudmore and James Lyons. The contracts specified that construction should commence by 1st April 1814 and the towers were to be completed by 1st April 1815 but this was to prove far too opti-

mistic. In March 1815 James Lyons complained that work 'cannot go ahead on Rossleague and Manning towers until roads have been built to the location of the towers' and, in fact, the towers were not completed until 1817.[7]

All five towers remained part of the defences of Cork Harbour until the 1870s and, in fact, the report of the Royal Commission on the Defences of the United Kingdom of 1860 actually recommended the construction of four further towers to defend Cork Harbour, three at Ballycotton Bay on the coast south east of Cork and one at Ringabella Bay on the western shore of the harbour. However, when steps were taken to reduce the huge cost of implementing the commissioner's report the plan to build these new towers was cancelled. However by 1874 only two towers, Ringaskiddy and Haulbowline, retained their armament which by that date was a single 32-pounder SBML gun in each tower.

For a number of years the towers were used as powder magazines and as married quarters for the gunners acting as caretakers and in 1867 Manning Tower at Marino Point on Great Island became the only Martello tower to be successfully attacked by an enemy force. In that year a number of members of the

Figure 6.7: The Rossleague tower on the northern side of Great Island. This tower is currently derelict. (*Author's photograph*).

Figure 6.8: Manning Tower on Marino Point, Great Island. This is the tower that was raided by a group of Fenians in 1867. (*Author's photograph*).

Fenian Brotherhood, an underground organization in Ireland opposed to British 'occupation' of the island, attacked the tower just as the two gunners and their families who lived in the tower were sitting down to supper. The Fenian group was led by a 'Captain Mackay' whose real name was William Francis Lomasney and they escaped with all the stores in the tower and 300 pounds (131 kg) of gunpowder from the magazine. Lomasney was to die seventeen years later in a failed attempt to blow up London Bridge.

Today the five towers still remain in varying states of repair. The tower on Haulbowline Island is in good condition and is now within the grounds of the Irish Navy base on the island and maintained by the Irish Navy. The tower at Belvelly Bridge, having stood derelict for many years, has now been converted very successfully and sympathetically into a private residence but the other three towers, Ringaskiddy, Rossleague and the tower at Marino Point, all lie derelict and in a poor state of repair.

Chapter 7

THE QUADRANGULAR TOWERS AND SIGNAL TOWERS

In addition to the Martello towers two other forms of small defensive works were built in Ireland between 1803 and 1816 during the war with Napoleon. These were the quadrangular towers and the defensible signal towers and both these types of structure were unique to Ireland. However, unlike the Martello towers which frequently stood alone unsupported by an adjoining battery the quadrangular tower was always to be found closing the gorge of a detached battery while the signal towers were designed simply for the protection of the signal party against an insurgent population.

Quadrangular Towers

In all a total of ten quadrangular towers were built in Ireland between 1809 and 1817; of these seven were built to defend the River Shannon which provided access to an invader to Limerick and the centre of the country. Six of these towers were constructed along the shores of the Shannon estuary below Limerick and one on the Upper Shannon to defend a ford at Keelogue below Athlone. Two others were built on the shores of Lough Swilly in County Donegal and one on Bere Island in Bantry Bay in County Cork.

The ten quadrangular towers were built as a result of the recommendations concerning the Irish defences made by the Committee of Engineers under Brigadier General Gother Mann in 1805-06. As early as 1797 General Valencey, the commander of the Royal Engineers in Ireland, had recommended batteries at Kilcredaun and Doonaha for the defence of the Shannon, and the members of the committee were clear in their opinion that the lower Shannon needed to be defended between Limerick and the sea and that this could best be done by siting batteries of heavy guns on both shores of the estuary.

The committee recommended that an existing battery on Tarbert Island on the southern shore of the estuary, Packenham Redoubt, should be improved and a tower built in the gorge of the battery. In addition, batteries and towers should be built at Kilcredaun Point on the northern shore and at Doonaha five miles (8km) to the east of Kilcredaun Point. Between Doonaha and Tarbert there were two islands opposite each other in the estuary, Scattery Island to the north and Carrig Island to the south and on each of these islands the committee recommended the construction of a battery and a tower. Finally, a battery was proposed for Kilkerin Point on the northern shore.

Although the committee's original proposals were for a round tower for each battery there was subsequent debate concerning the most appropriate design for the tower. On 9th May 1809 Colonel Fisher, the Commanding Royal Engineer in Dublin, wrote to Lieutenant Colonel Rowley, staff officer to the Inspector General of Fortifications in London, on the subject of the proposed batteries. 'Considering that the Towers and Batteries on the Lower Shannon will be at a distance from any support', he wrote, 'it may be adviseable [sic] to pay more than common attention to their Defence and to have them better secured from assault'.[1] Four months later Fisher wrote again seeking advice as to whether the lower Shannon towers should be round or square. The Inspector General replied: 'Respecting the question of square or round Tower – as

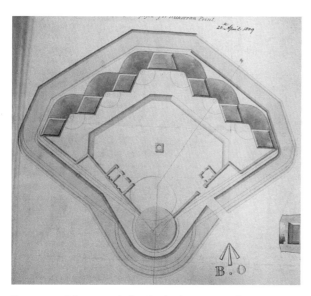

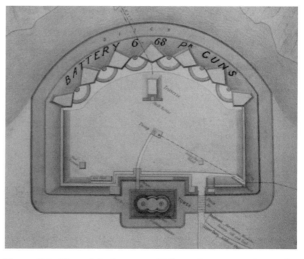

Figure 7.1: The original plan for the battery at Kilkerin Point showing the proposed circular tower. *(TNA MPHH 1/598).*

Figure 7.2: Plan of the battery at Kilkerin Point as constructed dated 1865. A quadrangular tower replaced the proposed circular tower and the plan shows the battery after its rearmament with six 68-pounder SB guns. *(TNA WO 78/4761).*

Figure 7.3: The quadrangular tower of the Corran Point battery. The tower is derelict and in poor condition. *(Author's photograph).*

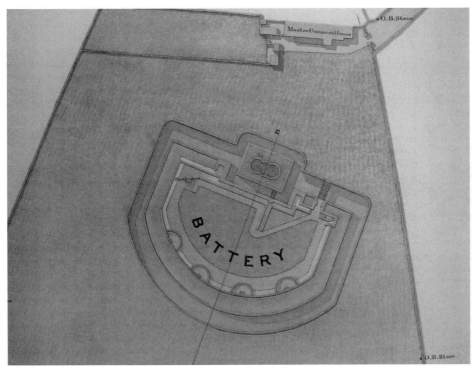

Figure 7.4: Plan of Doonaha quadrangular tower and battery. This battery, together with the battery at Kilcredaun Point, was abandoned in 1870. (TNA WO 78/4761).

they are designed to be joined to the Batteries, square Towers would in this case give greater protection than round ones'.[2] So rather than having a circular tower protecting the open gorge of a battery the Shannon batteries were to be small, self-contained forts surrounded by ditches with masonry scarp and counterscarp. In one case, that of the battery on Scattery Island, the ditch was defended by a counterscarp gallery entered from the *terreplein* of the battery.

The design of all these towers was basically similar with each being rectangular in shape and, like the Martello towers, comprising two storeys and a gun platform on top and averaging 30ft (9.2m) in height. Although the size of the towers varied slightly with that at Doonaha being the smallest, on the whole they averaged 52ft (16m) in length and 37ft (11.3m) in width with walls 9ft (2.75m) thick. The walls had a batter in the ratio 1:12. The quadrangular towers on the Shannon were built of limestone ashlar while those on the shores of Lough Swilly and the one on Bere Island were of granite. The Shannon towers were all surrounded by a ditch which varied in width from 13ft (4m) to 16ft (5m) and 10ft (3m) to 13ft (4m) in depth.

The quadrangular tower of the Western Redoubt on Bere Island in Bantry Bay and those at Rathmullen and Buncrana in County Donegal differed from the quadrangular towers on the Shannon by being surrounded on only three sides by the ditch. There was no ditch on the front face of the tower and entrance to the tower was directly from the battery *terreplein* at first floor level. The Shannon

Figure 7.5: Section of the quadrangular tower at Doonaha on the north shore of the of the Shannon Estuary. (*Author's collection*)

Figure 7.6: The tower at Doonaha Fort which is now in ruins. However, the photograph clearly shows the construction of the vaulted bomb-proof roof beneath the gun platform which has now disappeared. *(Author's photograph)*.

towers were also accessed from the *terreplein* but because the ditch extended along the front face of these towers access was by means of a drawbridge. The Lough Swilly quadrangular towers also differed from the others in the fact that the rear face of each projected outwards at a shallow angle towards the centre of the face giving them a pentagonal rather than rectangular form.

The basement of the tower contained the magazine, the capacity of which averaged 125 barrels of gunpowder, and three storerooms and in some towers there were musket loops in the walls providing defence for the ditch on either side of the guardhouse. At Ned's Point there were four musket loops in the NW wall and in the SE wall there was the unusual design of three musket loops accessed from a single firing position. The Rathmullen tower had four musket loops covering the main entrance to the fort.

The upper, or first, floor of these quadrangular towers was divided into two rooms, a large one capable of accommodating twenty men and the smaller for the officer in charge, and it had a barrel-vaulted bomb-proof roof. Communication between the two floors was by means of a stone staircase built into the rear wall. There was a window in each flank wall providing illumination for each room and there was also a fireplace in each room. Unusually, at Ned's Point the window is in the lower part of the tower overlooking the bottom of the ditch rather than at ground level as in other towers. It is possible that this window was inserted when the quadrangular tower was remodelled in 1897 and the height of the building reduced.

The armament of all the quadrangular towers comprised two 5½-in (140-mm) iron howitzers mounted on traversing platforms on the gun platform

Figure 7.7: Scattery Island quadrangular tower looking from the battery *terreplein* towards the tower. (*Author's photograph*).

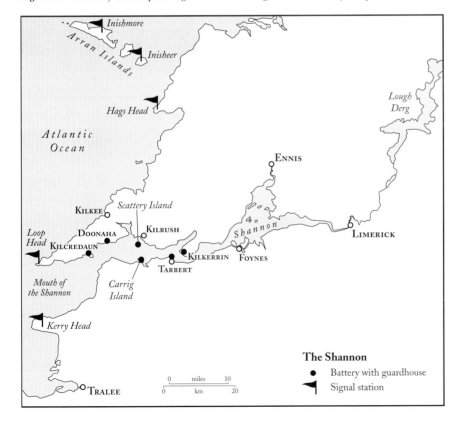

Figure 7.8: The Shannon towers and signal stations. (*Martin Brown*)

giving them each a traverse of 270 degrees. These howitzers were primarily for the defence of the battery rather than for an anti-shipping role which was the responsibility of the heavy guns on the battery *terreplein*. Once again, due to a lack of unserviceable guns that might act as pivots for the traversing platforms, it was necessary to manufacture the pivots locally. Unlike the majority of the Martello towers, the tower of the fort at Greencastle being an exception, the quadrangular towers had loopholes in the flank walls to enable musketry fire to be brought down on any enemy force penetrating into the ditch. Only in the Scattery tower were there loopholes at first floor level in the rear wall of the tower commanding the approach to the battery from the rear. In all the quadrangular towers there were loopholes at first floor level covering the battery *terreplein* indicating that it was envisaged that the tower would be a 'keep' or position of final defence.

In 1809 the decision was taken to substitute a quadrangular tower for the round tower at the Western Redoubt on Bere Island.[3] This was probably due to the poor standard of construction of the original round tower. The new tower was similar in design to the Lough Swilly quadrangular towers in only having a ditch on three sides and its original armament was to have been two 'short' 24-pounder SBML guns but this was subsequently changed to two 5½-in (140 mm) howitzers. The tower was built of granite ashlar lined with bricks and had perpendicular walls. Work on the tower commenced in 1810 but, once again, it would appear that the workmanship was poor; so poor indeed that the Commanding Royal Engineer was reporting a failure of the arches and stating that the defective part of the guardhouse must be taken down and rebuilt.[4] In 1812 it was taken down and rebuilt the following year.

The original estimate of the total cost for the works on the Lower Shannon made by the Committee of Engineers was £27,500 for the five new batteries and the rebuilding of Packenham Redoubt. However when accurate estimates were compiled and work commenced in 1811 the total cost came to £26,547 which says much for the professionalism of the Royal Engineer officers of the committee. The individual estimates for the batteries were as follows:

Figure 7.9: A section of the ditch surrounding the Scattery Island quadrangular tower. The photograph shows three of the gun loops in the rear wall of the tower and the gun loops in the counterscarp gallery. (*Author's photograph*).

Carrig Island (6 guns)	£4,572.10s.4d.
Doonaha Point (4 guns)	£4,100.0s.3d.
Kilcredaun Point (6 guns)	£5,111.0s.10d.
Kilkerin Point (6 guns)	£4,216.13s. 0d.
Packenham Redoubt (7 guns)	£3,875.16s.7d.
Scattery Island (6 guns)	£4,572.19s.0d.

The batteries and their quadrangular towers were completed over a period between 1812 and 1816. Ned's Point Battery at Buncrana in County Donegal was the first to be completed in 1812, at a cost of £5,450 4s.7¼ d.[5] and Keelogue Battery on the upper Shannon the last in 1816. The batteries at

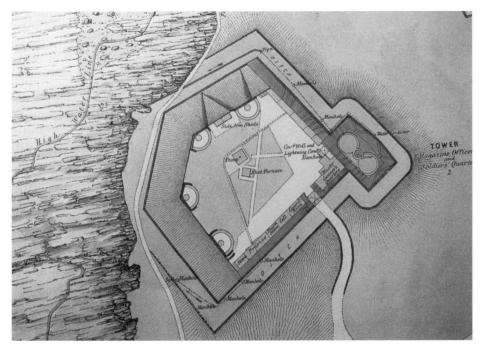

Figure 7.10: Plan of the quadrangular tower and battery at Ned's Point, Buncrana, on the shores of Lough Swilly. *(TNA WO 78/4759).*

Figure 7.11: An aerial view of Ned's Point Battery which clearly shows how the tower was subsequently remodelled and reduced in height in 1895 when the battery was re-armed with breech-loading guns. *(Author's collection).*

Figure 7.12: The quadrangular tower at Rathmullen Battery on Lough Swilly. The tower is now the Rathmullen Heritage Centre. (*Author's photograph*).

Kilcredaun Point and Scattery Island on the lower Shannon were complete in 1814 and Rathmullen Battery was completed the following year. Although these were the only quadrangular towers to be built three others were proposed but, in fact, never constructed. In 1810 there had been a proposal to build a quadrangular tower to defend the gorge of Battery Number 1 at Athlone at an estimated cost of

Figure 7.13: Rathmullen Battery showing one side of the quadrangular tower with the gun loops defending the ditch and the main gate. (*Author's photograph*).

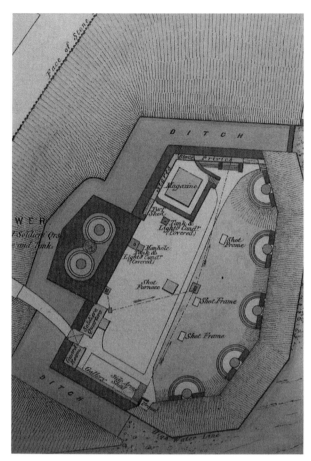

Figure 7.14: Plan of Rathmullen Battery in 1863. The battery retained its armament of five 24-pounder SB guns at that time. (*TNA WO 78/4759*).

Figure 7.15: The gun platform of the tower of Rathmullen Battery. The photograph shows the locally-made pivots for the two howitzers. (*Author's photograph*).

£2,600 but this was not proceeded with.[6] Nor was a similar proposal in 1811 for a quadrangular tower for Fort Carlisle to defend Cork Harbour nor one for Haulbowline Island, also in Cork Harbour, where a Martello tower was subsequently built.[7] Twenty years later, in 1830, there was a further proposal to build a quadrangular tower to defend the bridge across the Shannon at Portumna, south of Meelick, a major crossing that had not previously been permanently fortified. However, 1830 was a time of peace and there was no enthusiasm for this proposal!

The ten batteries all remained manned until the 1870s although the number of troops stationed at each was kept to a minimum. In 1835 the Master General of the Ordnance ordered that all batteries in Ireland not required for the protection of merchant

shipping (viz: those defending Cork Harbour, Dublin, Lough Foyle and the mouth of the Shannon) should be dismantled.[8] So the Shannon batteries each retained a garrison of gunners from the RA company stationed at Limerick which in 1831 comprised, according to the Clare Journal of 9th May that year, a total of 30 NCOs and gunners for the six batteries! In 1837, according to Samuel Lewis in his *Topographical Dictionary of Ireland*, the garrison of Ned's Point Fort near Buncrana in Donegal was a Master Gunner and five gunners from the Invalid Battalion RA. However, there was an interesting development in 1843 when the Shannon batteries were manned by a detachment of Royal Marines comprising two officers and 74 marines. The Royal Marines garrisoned the batteries for five years and this may have been related to the fact that the Admiralty had moorings at Tarbert and a number of Royal Navy warships were based on the Shannon.

In 1849 the Royal Marines garrisoning the batteries on the Shannon were replaced by a RA detachment of 37 NCOs and gunners. In 1859 personnel of the newly formed Coast Brigade RA replaced the old Invalid Battalion RA gunners when that unit was disbanded. Six years later, in 1870, the decision was taken to abandon the Kilcredaun Point and Doonaha batteries, probably as a result of the re-arming of the four remaining batteries with more powerful 68-pounder SBML guns. In 1873 the RA garrisons of the remaining batteries were replaced by a detachment from 2nd Battalion 20th (East Devonshire) Regiment.[9] This was not quite as surprising as it might seem since infantry regiments included the 'great gun' exercise in their training up until the start of the First World War. In 1880 two of the 68-pounder SBML guns at Kilkerin Point were replaced with 64-pounder RML guns but in 1889 the decision was finally taken to abandon all ten batteries

and the garrison finally left Scattery Island in the lower Shannon in 1891.

Fate has been relatively kind to the seven quadrangular towers on the Shannon as all but one still remain in reasonable condition except Doonaha which is now in ruins. Indeed, the Scattery Island battery was used by the Limerick Harbour Commissioners for their Western Pilots from 1875 until 1930 when a pilot house was built in the grounds of the battery. The one tower that has disappeared is that on Tarbert Island which was demolished in the 1950s to make way for an electricity generating station. The history of the other three towers, those on the shores of Lough Swilly and the one on Bere Island is rather more chequered. Only the quadrangular tower of the Rathmullen Battery on the western shore of Lough Swilly can still be seen today, now converted into the 'Flight of the Earls' Heritage Centre. In 1895 the battery at Ned's Point in Buncrana was converted to mount two 6-in (152mm) BL guns on hydro-pneumatic mountings and the tower was reduced in height and a depression

Figure 7.16: The tower of Keelogue Battery near Banagher on the Upper Shannon. *(Author's photograph).*

range-finder installed on top. On Bere Island the Western Redoubt was completely demolished to allow the construction of Reenduff Battery, a battery for two 4.7-in (120mm) QF guns, to be constructed on the site.

Signal Towers

The renewal of war with France in 1803 and the continued state of unrest in Ireland led, as we have seen in previous chapters, to the fortification of parts of the coast against invasion. Since the strength of the army in Ireland was insufficient to protect all those parts of the coast vulnerable to an enemy landing, it followed that early information of the arrival of an invasion force would be vital. This information could only be provided if there was an effective and fast method of communication linking Army headquarters in Dublin with the threatened parts of the coast.

In 1803 it had become clear to the Lord Lieutenant, Lord Hardwicke, that Ireland needed a chain of coastal signal stations similar to that along the south and east coasts of England. In a letter in June 1803 to the Rt Hon Lord Hawksbury, the

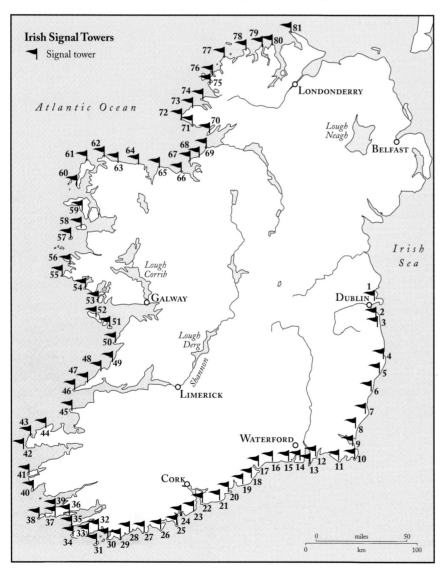

Figure 7.17: Irish signal towers. (*Martin Brown*)

Figure 7.18: The signal tower at Malin Head in County Donegal as drawn by Captain Sir William Smith, the Assistant Engineer at Lough Swilly in 1808. In addition to the tower the picture shows the signal mast and the original signal hut. (*Board of Trinity College, Dublin*).

Secretary of State for the Home Department, the Lord Lieutenant stated: 'The advantages arising from the establishment of a regular Service of Signal Stations on the Coast of Ireland similar to those which were erected on the East coast of England in the year 1798 were so clear and obvious that within a very short period after the renewal of the War I felt it my duty to bring the subject under the consideration of His Majesty's Ministers… And a plan has been actually settled for completing the whole of the communication, from Malin Head in the north by the western and southern coasts to Dublin.'[10] He requested the government in London to provide him with a naval adviser and, in the same year, the Admiralty instructed Rear Admiral Hawkins Whitshed RN to proceed to Dublin where he was to act as naval adviser to the Lord Lieutenant. While

being primarily responsible for the establishment of a force of Sea Fencibles, similar to that already established to defend the British coast, he also set up a line of signal towers from Dublin along the south and west coasts of Ireland to the end of the line at Malin Head the northernmost point in Ireland.

In August 1803 plans were authorised for the establishment of a number of signal stations and flag staffs in west Cork, probably linked to the establishment of a naval base in Bantry Bay for Rear Admiral Sir Robert Calder's squadron. However, in the next three years eighty one stations were established, one on every headland along the west coast from Malin Head south and east as far as Dublin. Each station was to be in visual contact with the stations on either side and signals were transmitted by means of three flags, a rectangular flag, a pennant and a narrow

Figure 7.19: The Malin Head signal tower today. The relatively intact state of the tower is largely due to its use as a Lloyd's of London signal station until a new radio station was built nearby in 1913. (*Author's photograph*).

triangular flag together with four black balls. By using these in varying combinations a limited number of simple prearranged messages could be passed between the stations or ships offshore. In poor weather conditions a beacon was to be lit in emergencies. However, the final positions of these towers were such that it would seem that visual communication between some towers was not always possible, even in good weather, due to the distance between the towers.

In addition to the signal towers three small defensible barracks were built in County Kerry, on Bolus Head and Hog's Head, the twin arms of Ballinskelligs Bay and on Kerry Head. A fourth barracks was built on Rough Point on the Magharees Peninsula on the north shore of the Dingle Peninsula. Two of the barracks, those on Bolus Head and Kerry Head were

built adjacent to the signal tower while the other two stood alone, though it appears that the Hog's Head barracks may have been originally intended to stand by a signal station that was never built. All the barracks were built to an identical design and comprised a rectangular walled enclosure 30yds long and 25yds wide (27m by 23m) with a small bastion at each corner and a strong stone-built two-storey house that formed part of the rear wall of the barracks. It is probable that these barracks were used to accommodate a small garrison with the double role of rotating the personnel guarding the nearby signal towers and acting in a policing role considering the unsettled state of the country at that time.

Although when first set up each station had only a wooden hut and signal mast it was decided that because of the isolated location of many of the stations and the unsettled state of large parts of the country the stations in these locations should be provided with a defensible stone building. In the end the majority of the signal stations were supplied with defensible towers but it would appear that at a few locations, in particular Ballygannon, Kilmichael Point and Cahore Point, all in County Wicklow, no tower was erected. On the Ordnance Survey map of 1840 only a flagstaff is marked at each place.

On 21st September 1803 Lieutenant Colonel Beckwith (secretary to the Commander-in-Chief in Ireland) wrote to Colonel Fisher RE explaining in detail what the Commander-in-Chief required: 'I am therefore to suggest the expediency of constructing at the stations where the signal posts may be found necessary, buildings of stone capable of lodging six men, with a distinct apartment for the officer, and defensible by that number.'[11] Indeed, Beckwith went on to suggest the construction of round towers about 20ft (6.16m) high, 'mounting two or three blunder-busses on swivel stocks'.[12] Since the object was stated as being 'merely defence against the attempts of the disaffected', it was felt there was no need to go to the expense of constructing Martello towers, though as we have seen two such towers were subsequently built in Wexford as part of the chain to act as combined gun towers and signal stations. Consideration was also given to constructing the proposed tower at Ballygannon, south of Dublin, as a Martello tower

Figure 7.20: Dromore West signal tower in County Sligo. The tower is in a relatively good state of repair and two of the *machicoulis* can be seen in the photograph. (*Author's photograph*).

but this idea was subsequently dropped.

Each signal station was manned by a Royal Navy lieutenant, usually one who was on half-pay, a midshipman and a signal party of two or three sailors. There is a record of the death of a Daniel Hamline at Creevagh signal tower in 1809 and it is possible that he was the Lieutenant Daniel Hamline who commanded the cutter HMS *Penelope* in 1799. The sailors were frequently found from the local Sea Fencible district. In addition, there was a small guard provided by the local Yeomanry or Fencible infantry regiment or, occasionally, from a nearby regular infantry battalion. The unsettled nature of conditions in Ireland necessitated the provision of a protection party and the signal station building was designed, in the words of Lieutenant Colonel Beckwith: 'to

prevent the destruction of the signal posts without the necessity of protecting them by strong detachments'[13]

Although the Commander-in-Chief's original suggestion was for round towers, the subsequent signal towers were eventually two-storey square towers. Edmund Wakefield, in *An Account of Ireland, Statistical and Political*, volume 2, published in 1812, describes one signal station – that at Kerry Head in County Kerry – as follows:

> The Signal Station consists of a square tower thirty four feet [10.46m] in height, each side of which is thirteen feet [4m] wide. It is committed to the care of a lieutenant and a guard. The door is in the upper storey, the only access to it by means of a small ladder, which can be handed up in a moment. It is built of stone and might be defended by half a dozen men against any number unless provided with cannon.

In fact, the towers varied somewhat in plan if not in height with some being as large as 19ft square and the walls could vary in thickness between two and four feet. The towers, with a few exceptions, all had a flat roof surrounded by a parapet from which projected three *machicoulis*, a large one over the doorway and two smaller ones on the rear corners of the parapet. To combat the notoriously wet Irish weather the walls of the towers were covered with hanging slates, though only one or two towers retain these slates today. A number of towers, including those at Mizen Head and Roberts Head in County Cork and the tower on Achill Island had pitched roofs covered with slates.

As described by Wakefield the entrance to the towers was through a door at first floor level and there were four windows in each side wall with the fourth wall having no openings. The windows were each protected by iron shutters. A large chimney was mounted on the rear wall of the roof parapet. There was accommodation for the RN lieutenant on the first floor, and access to the ground floor, where the small naval signal party and the army guard were accommodated, was by means of internal ladders. The guard was certainly necessary as the towers were, on occasions, subjected to attacks by the local peasantry and as late as 1816 the Public Accounts show the sum of £7.2s.½d. disbursed 'relative to Outrages and Attacks made on several Signal Towers in the County of Kerry'.[14]

Each tower was surrounded by a stone wall forming a rectangular enclosure with a fan-shaped extension on the seaward side that acted as a form of defensive perimeter. In the centre of the extension there was a post hole for a signal mast. In a number of locations, however, that were particularly difficult to access, such as Carrigan Head in Donegal, there was no enclosure while on Loop Head at the mouth of the Shannon the tower is sited in a large ring fort.

The signal stations were numbered from No.1 at Pigeon House Fort in Dublin to No.81 at Malin Head in County Donegal. Of this total 77 were towers, the signal stations in Dublin, at Rosslare and Baginbun Head in Wexford and at Hog's Head in Cork being established in a fort, two Martello towers and a small

barracks respectively. Work started on the towers in 1804 and most were completed by 1806 though by that year the Dursey Island tower was reported as only having bare walls standing; in 1811 it was not roofed or glazed; and in 1812 was said not to be in an inhabitable state. There seems a strong possibility that this particular tower was never occupied. The average cost of each tower was approximately £600 though where the locations were difficult to access the cost increased and the tower on Carrigan Head, on the spectacular Slieve League cliffs in County Donegal, cost £690 to build.

The limited capability of the towers to communicate with each other meant that there was little enthusiasm for maintaining them once the immediate threat of invasion was past. In 1809 Admiral Whitshed was instructed to abandon 48 of the stations, leaving only Nos 23 to 51 between Cork

Figure 7.21: The tower at Carrigan Head, County Donegal. The tower is sited on the edge of the Slieve League cliffs and is a good example of the remote and difficult location in which many of these towers were sited. (*Author's photograph*).

Figure 7.22: Map of the ground occupied by the signal tower at Galley Head, County Cork in 1806. *(NLI 14244).*

and Inisheer Island in Galway Bay, and the Melmore, Fanad and Malin Head towers at the entrance to Lough Swilly remaining in operation. Although some of the abandoned stations were reactivated during the war with the United States from 1812 to 1815, all were finally abandoned by 1816, a number having been occupied by families up to that date. By 1842 many, including the Loop Head tower, were shown on the Ordnance Survey map as already being in ruins.

The towers were never again used as signal towers with the exception of the Malin Head and Sybil Head towers. The Malin Head tower was used for many years by Lloyd's of London as a reporting station and has now been partially restored. The tower on Sybil Head was reconstructed in 1907 with a flat roof and a concrete first floor supported by steel joists and in the Second World War it was used as a coast-watching post by the Irish Defence Force.

Today the majority of the towers stand derelict and in ruins and, in some locations, only heaps of stone remain to mark where a tower once stood. However, the tower at Lamcom in County Cork has now been converted into a private dwelling with consideration for its original design. The *machicoulis* have been glazed but otherwise the conversion is, from the exterior, true to the original. The same cannot be said for the Ardmore tower in County Waterford where the tower has been castellated, the *machicoulis* removed and the whole given a cement rendering. Toe Head, also in County Cork, is another tower that has, at some period, been castellated and a two-storey building added to it, probably in the 1820s when it was a coastguard station. Other towers used by the coastguards with additional buildings included Roberts Head and Mizen Head in County Cork and the Ballard tower near Doonbeg in County Clare.

Although the towers themselves were abandoned some of their locations were to come into use once again during the First World War when Naval War Signal stations were established by the Royal Navy at Galley Head, Loop Head, Mizen Head, Cahermore, Bray Head and Sybil Head. In the Second World

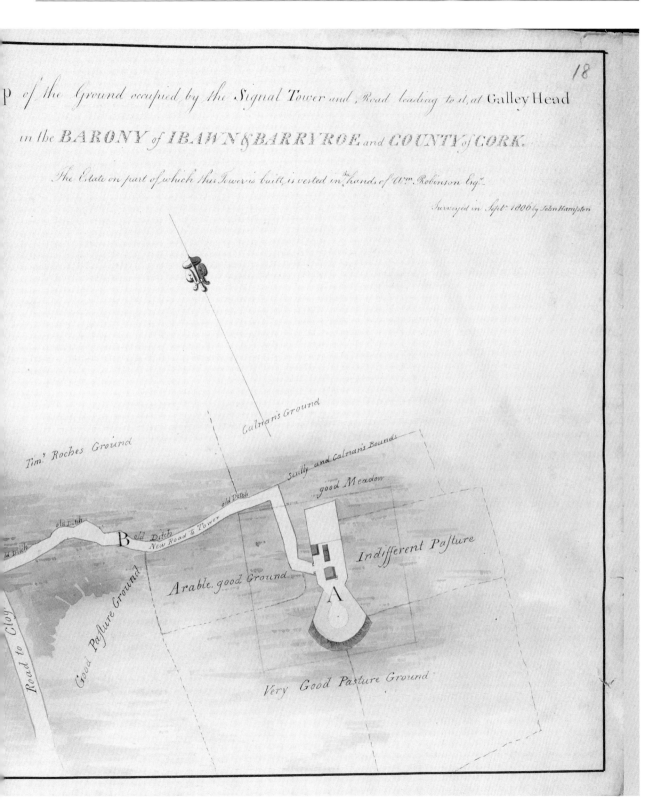

p of the Ground occupied by the Signal Tower and Road leading to it, at Galley Head

in the BARONY of IBAWN & BARRYROE and COUNTY of CORK.

The Estate on part of which this Tower is built, is vested in the hands of Wm. Robinson Esq.

Surveyed in Sept. 1806 by John Hampston

Calnan's Ground

Tim.r Roches Ground

Scully and Calnan's Bounds

old Ditch

good Meadow

old Ditch

old Ditch

B old Ditch
New Road to Tower

Indifferent Pasture

Arable good Ground

A

Good Pasture Ground

Road to Cloy

Very Good Pasture Ground

Figure 7.23:
Letterbeg signal tower at Blacksod Point in County Mayo. (*Author's photograph*).

War, or 'The Emergency' as it was known in Ireland, between 1940 and 1945 the Eire government set up a Coast-watching Service to enable it to maintain its neutrality. In most locations where the Napoleonic towers had been constructed a small concrete observation post was built alongside the Napoleonic towers and many of these can still be seen today.

Although most towers are now in ruins or derelict recently it would appear that there has been a greater appreciation of their historic importance and efforts are being made to maintain and refurbish them as demonstrated by the development of the tower at the Old Head of Kinsale as a visitor and exhibition centre for the newly established Lusitania Memorial Garden.

CONCLUSION

The construction of the Martello towers and quadrangular towers in Ireland took place over the comparatively short period of fourteen years from 1804 to 1817 and cost in excess of £250,000, a sum that would equate to £50,000,000 today. More than fifty Martello towers and ten quadrangular towers were built in Ireland to meet a threat that never eventuated. However, as a deterrent to a French invasion, which, in fact, never materialised, it may be said that they were a success and perhaps worth the vast sum that was invested in their construction.

The Board of Ordnance was fortunate in having a group of talented officers of the Royal Engineers serving in Ireland. This group was led by Colonel (later Major General) Benjamin Fisher and included Lieutenant Colonel Fenwick and Captains Birch, Wright, Cardew and DeButts. All became prominent in their Corps in later years and Captain DeButts was to be knighted and retire as Colonel Commandant of the Royal Engineers. As a result a number of towers in Ireland were built to designs unique to the island including those towers designed to mount two heavy guns. In addition, the quadrangular towers were also unique to Ireland and all of these were designed during Fisher's period as Commanding Royal Engineer in Dublin.

The Martellos towers and other towers in Ireland had a limited span of operational life. By the middle of the nineteenth century advances in the design of artillery and artillery ammunition resulted in brick and stone fortifications becoming obsolete. However, as late as 1859 three towers were proposed for the defence of Youghal and Ballycotton Bay in Co Cork in the Royal Commission Report on the Defences of the United Kingdom but they were never built and at the time of the Fenian Rebellion in the 1860s five fortified Coastguard stations were constructed, each with an integral fortified tower.

Some Martello towers remained occupied, either by pensioners or soldiers and their families, until the end of the century when most were sold off, leased or simply allowed to become derelict through lack of basic maintenance.

However, on the whole the years have been relatively kind to the Irish towers when compared to similar structures in England with only nine Martello towers and two quadrangular towers having disappeared completely. Of this total three Martello towers have been destroyed by sea erosion, always a danger where structures are built close to the sea; four were demolished by the War Office when more modern fortifications were built on their sites; and two near Dublin were demolished, one to make way for a railway line. In addition, one quadrangular tower was demolished by the War Office to permit the construction of a modern breech-loading battery and another was demolished as recently as 1969 to enable a power station to be built on the site.

Today there is a greater interest in the fortifications of Ireland generally and the Martello towers are gradually being restored and refurbished, many as private residences and some as museums or simply as historic monuments and are open to the public. However, and sadly, the unique quadrangular towers have not fared so well and only one, the tower at Rathmullen on the shore of Lough Swilly in County Donegal, has been restored and converted into a heritage and visitor centre. The remainder are derelict and their condition is slowly deteriorating.

Although some of the Martello towers have been sympathetically restored many have not! The tower at Balbriggan, north of Dublin, is in a state of total dereliction; others, such as the tower at Malahide, known as 'Hick's Castle' and also north of Dublin, have been totally unsympathetically 'restored'; and a few, such as the Ardagh tower on Bere Island, Tower

No.7 at Killiney, south of Dublin, Tower No.14, also south of Dublin, and the tower at Magilligan Point in County Londonderry have, in contrast, been restored almost to their original condition.

So, although it is encouraging that steps are being taken to restore and preserve these important military heritage sites more could be done, particularly by both state and local government planning authorities. There have been too many instances of inappropriate conversion to residences that have ignored and, in some cases, destroyed the historical integrity of the building, although an outstanding exception is Tower No.10, south of Dublin. This tower has been refurbished by an architect, Simone Stephenson, in a way that combines modern design without permanently destroying the integrity of the tower. The Dun Laoghaire-Rathdown County Council is also to be congratulated on the interest it is taking in the Dublin Martello towers. In contrast, at Greencastle Fort on the shore of Lough Foyle, although the Martello tower is still intact, a developer has been permitted to destroy a rare magazine and bulldoze the lower battery to make space for houses.

It is quite possible to convert the Martello towers to other uses without destroying the historical integrity of these structures and every effort should be made to ensure that this is done. This is the responsibility of the Irish Government's Department of the Arts, Heritage and the Gaeltacht and of the Environment Agency Built Heritage Department in Northern Ireland, but it is also the responsibility of owners and their architects. It is to these individuals and organisations that we must look if we are to preserve these historic structures.

Annex A

MARTELLO TOWERS
LOCATION AND DESCRIPTION

Tower	Location	Date	Diam. (ft)	Height (ft)	Plan	Original armament	Comments
Dublin North							
1	Sutton Creek O267372	1804-06	38	30	circ	1 x 24pdr gun	now three apartments
2	Howth O288393	1804-06	38	30	circ	1 x 24pdr gun	Antique radio museum
3	Ireland's Eye O284416	1804-06	55	30	circ	2 x 24pdr guns	Disused
4	Carrick Hill, Portmarnock O249445	1804-	38	30	circ	1 x 24pdr gun	now a house
5	Robswall, Malahide O240457	1804-06	38	30	circ	1 x 24pdr gun	Hick's Castle
6	Balcarrick O253493	1804-06	38	30	circ	1 x 24pdr gun	Derelict
7	Portrane O264505	1804-06	38	30	circ	1 x 24pdr gun	now a house
8	Rush O277541	1804-06	38	30	circ	1 x 24pdr gun	Disused
9	Drumanagh O275563	1804-06	38	30	circ	1x24pdr gun	Derelict
10	Shenick's Is O268599	1804-	38	30	circ	1 x 24pdr gun	Derelict
11	Red Island, Skerries O257611	1804-06	38	30	circ	1 x 24pdr gun	owned by Fingal County Council
12	Balbriggan O203645	1804-	38	30	circ	1 x 24pdr gun	Derelict

Tower	Location	Date	Diam. (ft)	Height (ft)	Plan	Original armament	Comments
Dublin South							
1	Bray Head O273185	1804-06	38	30	circ	1 x 18pdr gun	Destroyed by sea erosion
2	Bray Point O269191	1804-06	38	30	circ	1 x 18pdr gun	now a house
3	Cork Abbey O267195	1804-06	40	30	circ	1 x 18pdr gun	Destroyed
4	Maghera Point O264218	1804-06	40	30	circ	1 x 18pdr	Demolished by British Army 1906
6	Loughlinstown O260238	1804-06	38	30	circ	1 x 18pdr gun	now a house
7	Tara Hill, Killiney O257245	1804-06	38	30	circ	1 x 18pdr gun	now restored
9	Dalkey Island O278263	1804-06	50	35	circ	2 x 24pdr guns	Derelict
10	Bullock O266276	1804-06	40	30	circ	1 x 18pdr gun	now a house
11	Sandycove O259281	1804-06	42	30	circ	1 x 18pdr gun	now James Joyce Museum
12	Glasthule, Dun Laoghaire O248283	1804-	38	30	circ	1 x 18pdr gun	Destroyed
13	Dun Laoghaire O237287	1804-06	38	30	circ	1 x 18pdr gun	Destroyed
14	Seapoint O228291	1804-06	42	30	circ	1 x 18pdr gun	Restored and open to the public
15	Seafort Pde, Williamstown O208300	1804-06	50	30	circ	2 x 24pdr guns	Disused
16	Sandymount O195320	1804-06	50	30	circ	2 x 24pdr guns	Disused
Co.Wexford							
Fort Point Tower	Rosslare	1804-06	42	33	circ	1 x 24pdr carronade	Destroyed by sea erosion
Baginbun Tower	Baginbun Head T804033	1804-06	42	33	circ	1 x 24pdr	now a house
1	Duncannon S734085	1814-15	48	33	elip	1 x 24pdr gun	Disused
2	Duncannon S735087	1814-15	48	33	elip	1 x 24pdr	now a house

Tower	Location	Date	Diam. (ft)	Height (ft)	Plan	Original armament	Comments
Co.Cork							
Manning Tower	Marino Point Great Island Cork Harbour W782705	1813-15	48	37	circ	1 x 24pdr gun	Disused
Belvelly Tower	Belvelly, Great Island, Cork Harbour W791707	1813-15	48	37	circ	1 x 24pdr gun	now a house
Ringaskiddy Tower	Crosshaven, Cork Harbour W787639	1813-15	52	–	oval	1 x 24pdr gun	Derelict
Rossleague Tower	Great Island, Cork Harbour W810701	1813-15	44	32	circ	1 x 24pdr gun	Derelict
Haulbowline Tower	Haulbowline Island, Cork Harbour W789654	1813-15			circ	1 x 24pdr gun	In the care of the Irish Naval Service
Garinish Tower	Garinish Island Glengariff Harbour V935548	1804-06	37	34	circ	1 x 24pdr gun	Rebuilt. Now in the care of The Irish Board of Public Works and open to the public
Manly Tower (No.1)	Bere Island, Bantry Bay V761448	1804-06	38	28	circ	2 x 24pdr guns	Demolished by British Army 1897
Cathcart Tower (No.2)	Bere Island, Bantry Bay V757446	1804-06	38	28	circ	2 x 24pdr guns	Demolished by British Army 1897
Clochlan Tower (No.3)	Bere Island, Bantry Bay V732427	1804-06	38	28	circ	1 x 24pdr gun	Derelict
Ardagh Tower (No.4)	Bere Island, Bantry Bay V722439	1804-06	38	28	circ	1 x 24pdr gun	Restored
Co.Galway							
Rossaveel Tower	Cashla Bay L958234	1810-12	45	33	elip	1 x 24pdr gun 1 x 8-in how	Derelict
Meelick Tower	Meelick N946155	1812-15	55	33	cam	1 x 24pdr gun 2 x 5½-in hows	Derelict

Tower	Location	Date	Diam. (ft)	Height (ft)	Plan	Original armament	Comments
Co.Clare							
Aughinish Tower	Nr Kinvara M287136	1810-14	60	33	cam	1 x 24pdr gun 2 x 5½-in hows	now a house
Finavarra Tower	Nr Kinvara M241117	1810-14	55	33	cam	1 x 24pdr gun 2 x 5½-in hows	maintained by Irish Board of Public Works
Co.Offaly							
Fanesker Tower	Banagher N004161	1810-12	44	33	elip	1 x 24pdr gun	Disused
Co Donegal							
East Fort	Dunree Head Lough Swilly C285389	1810-15	18	28	circ	2 x 24pdr guns	Demolished by British Army 1897
West Fort	Lough Swilly C273371	1810-15	65	35	cam	1 x 24pdr gun 1 x 5½-in how	Privately owned
Macamish Battery	Lough Swilly C305325	1810-15	52	35	circ	2 x 24pdr guns	Privately owned, now a holiday home
Down of Inch Fort	Lough Swilly C309264	1810-15	55	33	cam	3 x 5½-in hows	Demolished by British Army 1897
Greencastle Fort	Lough Foyle C653403	1812-15	65	48	oval	2 x 24pdr carronades	Disused
Co Londonderry							
Magilligan Tower	Magilligan Pt Lough Foyle C661388	1812-15	55	36	circ	2 x 24pdr guns	Restored and open to the public
Co.Louth							
Richmond Fort Drogheda	Millmount, O088754	1808	40	37	circ	nil	Restored and open to the public

Annex B

CIRCULAR REDOUBTS AND QUADRANGULAR TOWERS

Tower	Location	Date	Dim (ft)	Height (ft)	Armament	Comments
Co.Cork						
Central Redoubt	Whiddy Island, Bantry Bay V973502	1804-06	250	–	12 x 24pdr guns	Circular redoubt. Derelict.
East Redoubt	Whiddy Island, Bantry Bay V977513	1804-06	210	–	8 x 24pdr guns	Circular redoubt. Derelict.
West Redoubt	Whiddy Island, Bantry Bay V946487	1804-06	210	–	8 x 24pdr guns	Circular redoubt. Derelict.
Western Redoubt	Bere Island Bantry Bay V680440	1804-06	250	–	2 x 5½-in hows	Quadrangular tower. Demolished
Co.Donegal						
Ned's Point Battery	Buncrana, Lough Swilly C335327	1810-15	53x40	35	2 x 5½-in hows	Quadrangular tower. Re-modelled 1897. Derelict
Rathmullen Battery	Rathmullen, Lough Swilly C299275	1810-15	55x37	35	2 x 5½-in hows	Quadrangular tower. Now a museum.
Co.Offaly						
Keelogue Battery	Inchkerky, Banagher N954154	1810-16	54x32	35	2 x 5½-in hows	Quadrangular tower. Derelict.

Tower	Location	Date	Dim (ft)	Height (ft)	Armament	Comments
Co.Clare						
Donaha Battery	Doonaha, Nr Kilrush Q886529	1810-14	50x34	35	2 x 5½-in hows	Quadrangular tower. In ruins.
Kilcredaun Battery	Kilcredaun Point Nr Kilrush Q850494	1810-14	52x32	35	2 x 5½-in hows	Quadrangular tower. derelict.
Kilkerin Battery	Kilkerin Point Nr Labasheeda Q095507	1810-14	58x37	35	2 x 5½-in hows	Quadrangular tower. Derelict.
Scattery Island Battery	Scattery Island Nr Kilrush Q972515	1810-14	53x32	35	2 x 5½-in hows	Quadrangular tower. Derelict.
Co.Limerick						
Corran Point Battery	Corran Point Carrig Island Q977486	1810-14	55x33	35	2 x 5½-in hows	Quadrangular tower. Derelict.
Tarbert Island Battery	Tarbert Island Tarbert GR Q076495	1810-14	55x35	35	2 x 5½-in hows	Quadrangular tower. Demolished.

Annex C

IRISH SIGNAL TOWERS & STATIONS

Number	Location	Condition	Grid Reference
1	Pigeon House Fort, Dublin	Demolished	O205337
	Dalkey Hill, Dublin	Restored	O261255
3	Ballygannon	Flagstaff	not known
4	Wicklow Head	Demolished	O345925*
5	Mizen Head, Wicklow	Ruined	O309805
6	Kilmichael Point	Flagstaff #	Unknown
7	Cahore Point	Demolished	T225474*
8	Blackwater Head	Demolished	T139325
9	Fort Point Martello tower	Demolished	T099187
10	Hill Castle	Unknown	T092107*
11	Crossfarnoge (Forlorn Point)	Demolished	S965035
12	Baginbun Head Martello tower	Now a house	T804033
13	Hook Head	Ruined	X738987*
14	Brownstone Head	Demolished	X613978*
15	Islandikane	Demolished	X534982
16	Bunmahon	Demolished	X447987*
17	Ballyvoyle Head	Ruined	X344950*
18	Ballynamona (Mine Head)	Ruined	X285828*
19	Ardmore (Ram Head)	Restored	X199768
20	Knockadoon Head	Derelict	X088695
21	Ballymacotter	Restored (now a house)	W954626
22	Roche's Point	Derelict	W825601
23	Roberts Head	Derelict	W782540
24	Barry's Head	Demolished	W727500
25	Old Head of Kinsale	Restored	W625409
26	Seven Heads	Derelict	W505355
27	Galley Head	Ruined	W372349
28	Glandore Head	Demolished	W249333
29	Toe Head	Derelict	W153269
30	Kedge Point (Ballylinchy)	Derelict	V060254
31	Cape Clear	Derelict	V968212
32	Lamcon	Restored (now a house)	V886298
33	Brow Head	Derelict	V778238

Number	Location	Condition	Grid Reference
34	Mizen Head, Cork	Derelict	V741239
35	Sheep's Head	Demolished	V743344
36	Bere Island	Demolished	V688433
37	Black Ball Head	Derelict	V587394
38	Dursey Island	Derelict	V474404
39	Bolus Head	Ruined	V388625
40	Bray Head, Valencia Island	Derelict	V331731
41	Great Blasket Island	Demolished	V271970
42	Sybil Head	Ruined	Q314063
43	Ballydavid	Ruined	Q387114
44	Brandon Head	Ruined	Q482146*
45	Kerry Head	Ruined	Q695318
46	Loop Head	Demolished	Q679472
47	Knocknagarhoon	Demolished	Q815551
48	Ballard Hill	Demolished	Q909659
49	Mutton Island	Ruined	Q967746
50	Hag's Head	Derelict	R013896
51	Inisheer,	Derelict	L983017
52	Inishmore,	Ruined	L861099
53	Golam Head,	Derelict	L818214
54	Lettermullan Island	Derelict	L827215
55	Ard Castle	Derelict	L752313*
56	Slyne Head	Demolished	L515411
57	Inishturk, Aran Islands	Ruined	L606753
58	Clare Island	Ruined	L652854
59	Achill Island	Ruined	F617074
60	Termon Hill (Glosh)	Ruined	F608197
61	Belmullet (Slievemore)	Demolished	F724360
62	Benwee Head (Benmore)	Demolished	F813432
63	Glinsk	Ruined	G950417
64	Creevagh	Demolished	G176404*
65	Rathlee	Derelict	G314388
66	Carrowmably (Dromore)	Derelict	G427350
67	Knocklane Hill	Demolished	G564447
68	Stridagh (Streedagh)	Demolished	G631507*
69	Killcologue Point (Mullaghmore)	Demolished	G704577*
70	St John's Point	Demolished	G706692
71	Carrigan Head	Derelict	G562749
72	Malin Beg	Derelict	G489796
73	Glen Head	Derelict	G519869
74	Dawros Head	Ruined	G639978
75	Crohy Head	Derelict	B708084
76	Mullaghderg Hill	Ruined	B750209
77	Bloody Foreland	Ruined	B818335
78	Horn Head	Ruined	C015417

Number	Location	Condition	Grid Reference
79	Melmore Head	Ruined	C137451
80	Fanad Head	Demolished	C231465
81	Malin Head	Derelict	C398596

Grid references are given using the Ordnance Survey Ireland *Discovery* series 1:50 000 scale maps.
An asterisk against a grid reference indicates the approximate position of a tower.
# indicates flagstaff only as shown on the 1840 Ordnance Survey map

NOTES

MAD –   Military Archives, Dublin
NAM –   National Army Museum, London
NLI ⁊   National Library of Ireland, Dublin
PRONI⁊   Public Records Office, Northern Ireland, Belfast
TCD ⁊   Trinity College Library, Dublin
TNA ⁊   The National Archives, Kew, London
Dippam –   Documenting Ireland: Parliament, People & Migration

Introduction
1. TNA WO 30/73

Chapter 1 – The Bantry Towers
1. TNA WO 55/832
2. ibid.
3. TNA WO 55/835
4. TNA WO 55/837
5. TNA WO 33/10
6. NLI Kilmainham Papers Ms.1119
7. TNA HO 100/121
8. TNA HO 100/120
9. TNA WO 55/831
10. PRONI T3465/154
11. PRONI T3465/168
12. TNA WO 55/831
13. ibid.
14. ibid.
15. ibid.
16. TNA HO 100/155
17. NAM, Alcock, Lt. Alex., RA, *Bere Island in Bantry Bay with a Review of its Effective Powers as a Fortified Place*, unpublished notebook, 1824 (NAM Archives, Acc.No.8409-11)
18. NLI Ms.4707
19. TNA WO 78/4759
20. TNA HO 100/155
21. NLI Ms.1122
22. TNA WO 55/838
23. TNA WO 396/1
24. TNA WO 396/4

Chapter 2 – The Dublin Towers
1. TNA WO 55/831
2. ibid.
3. MAD Plan & Section of Dalkey Tower
4. TNA WO 55/835
5. TNA WO 55/2685
6. TNA WO 44/109
7. TNA WO 396/1
8. TNA WO 55/836

Chapter 3 – The Towers of Lough Swilly & Lough Foyle
1. TNA WO 55/831
2. TNA WO 55/832 & 833
3. TNA WO 55/833
4. TCD Ms.942 Vol II f.190
5. TNA WO 55/247
6. TNA WO 44/109
7. TNA WO 55/849
8. TNA WO 55/832
9. TNA WO 55/833
10. TNA WO 55/835
11. Col George Lewis RE,'Report on the Application of Forts, Towers and Batteries to Coast Defences and Harbours', *Professional Papers of the Royal Engineers*, Vol VII,1844
12. TNA WO 55/833
13. Ordnance Survey of Ireland, *Memoirs of Ireland, Vol II, Parishes of County Londonderry III, 1831-35* (Belfast: Queen's University, Institute of Irish Studies, 1991), p.85
14. TNA WO 396/1

Notes

Chapter 4 – The Galway & Shannon Towers

1. Hardiman, James *The History of the Town & County of Galway*, W.Folds & Sons, Dublin 1820, p.176
2. ibid. p.281
3. NLI Ms.175 f.592
4. TNA WO 55/833
5. TNA WO 78/2785
6. TNA WO 55/833
7. TNA WO 55/836
8. TNA WO 55/833
9. TNA WO 33/5

Chapter 5 – The Wexford & Louth Towers

1. TNA HO 100/120
2. NLI Ms.4707
3. ibid.
4. ibid.
5. TNA WO 55/833
6. TNA WO 55/831
7. TNA WO 55/832
8. TNA WO 55/834

Chapter 6 – The Cork Towers

1. TNA WO 55/834
2. ibid.
3. ibid.
4. TNA WO 55/833
5. TNA WO 55/832
6. TNA WO 55/833
7. TNA WO 55/834

Chapter 7 – The Quadrangular Towers & Signal Towers

1. TNA WO 55/833
2. ibid.
3. ibid.
4. TNA WO 55/834
5. TNA WO 55/833
6. TNA WO 55/834
7. TNA WO 55/833
8. TNA WO 55/837
9. Freeman's Journal: Military Intelligence, 30th May 1873
10. TNA HO 100/120
11. NLI Kilmainham Papers, Ms.119 ff.368-9
12. ibid.
13. ibid.
14. Dippam, EPPI, HC 154 Sixth Report of the Commissioners for Auditing Public Accounts in Ireland,1816.

BIBLIOGRAPHY

Books & Booklets

Bolton, J. & others, *The Martello Towers of Dublin*, Dun Laoghaire-Rathdown CC & Fingal CC, Dublin 2012

Clements, W.H., *Towers of Strength*, Pen & Sword Books Ltd, Barnsley, 1999

Clements, W.H., *Defending the North: the fortifications of Ulster 1796-1956*, Colourpoint Books, Newtownards, 2003

Clements, W.H., *Martello Towers Worldwide*, Pen & Sword Books Ltd, Barnsley, 2011

Enoch, V.J., *The Martello Towers of Ireland*, Eason & Son (Distributor), Dublin 1975

Kerrigan, P.M., *Castles and Fortifications in Ireland 1485-1945*, The Collins Press, Cork 1995

McEnery, J.H., *Fortress Ireland*, Wordwell Ltd, Bray 2006

Ordnance Survey of Ireland, *Memoirs of Ireland*, Vol. 11, *Parishes of Co. Londonderry III, 1831-1835*, Queen's University of Belfast, Institute of Irish Studies, Belfast 1994

Ordnance Survey of Ireland, *Memoirs of Ireland*, Vol. 38, *Parishes of Co. Donegal I, 1833-1835*, Queen's University of Belfast, Institute of Irish Studies, Belfast 1997

Sutcliffe, Sheila, *Martello Towers*, David & Charles, Newton Abbot 1972

Articles

Cn, 'The Martello Towers of Cork Harbour', *Cork Historical & Archaeological Journal*, Series 2, Vol XIII, 1907

Donnelly, Morwenna, 'A Napoleonic Fort in Donegal', *Country Life*, 25th September 1975

Horner, Arnold, 'John Murray and the building of the Dun Laoghaire Martello towers', *The Irish Sword* (Journal of the Military History Society of Ireland), No.98 Vol. XXIV, Winter 2005

Kerrigan, P.M., 'The Defences of Ireland 2: The Martello Towers', *An Cosantoir* (Journal of the Irish Defence Force) May 1974

Kerrigan, P.M.,'Minorca and Ireland – an architectural connection; the Martello Towers of Dublin Bay', *The Irish Sword* (Journal of the Military History Society of Ireland), Vol. XV, Summer 1983

O'Brien, Comdt B.M., 'Martello Towers', *An Cosantoir* Vol. XXV No.7, July 1965

Stevenson, I.V., 'The Defences of Cork Harbour', *Fort* (Journal of the Fortress Study Group), Vol.27 1999

GLOSSARY

Amusette	long-barrelled, small-calibre wall gun (1 or 2-pounder)
Ashlar	square-hewn masonry blocks
Banquette	An infantry firing step.
Barbette	position in which guns are mounted to fire over a parapet rather than through embrasures in the parapet wall
Batter	inward slope of the surface of a wall
BL	breech-loading
Caponier	covered passage constructed across, or projecting into a ditch to provide sheltered communication across the ditch or to defend it
Carronade	large-calibre, short-barrelled, smooth-bore gun
Coehorn	small, portable mortar
Corbel	projection of stone, timber, etc. jutting out from a wall to support the weight of an overhanging construction
Cordon	stone string course at the top of a wall or part way up a wall
Counterscarp	outer wall of a ditch
Counterscarp Gallery	vaulted chamber constructed in the counterscarp in order to defend the ditch
Cunette	narrow moat in the middle of dry ditch, built to improve Drainage
Curtain	main wall of a fortified place that runs between the towers, bastions or gates
Embrasure	opening in a parapet or wall through which a gun can be fired
Enfilade	fire from artillery or musketry which sweeps a line of works or men from one end to the other
Epaulement	a raised wall giving additional

	protection to the rear of a Tower or gun position
Glacis	open slope extending from the ditch giving a clear field of fire to the defenders and partially covering the wall of the defended position from artillery fire
Gorge	the rear of a defended position or battery
Grillage	a heavy framework of cross-timbering, sometimes resting on the heads of piles, serving as a foundation for a building on watery or treacherous soil
Howitzer	A short-barrelled gun capable of firing shells at a high angle.
Keep	central tower of a fort or castle serving as a position of last defence
Machicoulis	a gallery projecting from the wall with openings between the corbels through which musketry fire can be brought to bear on an enemy at the base of the wall
OP	Observation Post
Parapet	breastwork designed to give the defenders on a wall or tower cover from fire and observation
Pas de Souris	staircase giving access to a ditch
Place d'armes	An open space for assembling troops.
QF	quick-firing
Quatrefoil	four-cusped figure resembling a four-leafed clover
Racer	circular or semi-circular, horizontal metal rail along which the wheels of a traversing platform for a gun moves
Redoubt	A type of outwork built of earth or

masonry in a square or polygonal shape with little or no means of flanking defence. A chain of redoubts consists of detached works designed to support each other.

Render (to)   to cover with a coat of plaster

RBL   rifled breech-loading

RML   rifled muzzle-loading: a type of gun in use between 1850 and 1890, just before the introduction of breech-loading guns

Sallyport   passage or gate giving access to the ditch for use by the defenders when making a counterattack

SB   smooth-bore

SBML   Smooth-bore muzzle-loading.

Stucco   coarse plaster or cement used to cover the exterior surface of a wall

Terreplein   surface of a rampart on which guns are mounted

Tete de Pont   fortification defending the approaches to a bridge

Traverse   a raised bank or wall to protect defenders from enfilade fire

Trefoil   three-cusped figure resembling a shamrock

Wallpiece   small, muzzle-loading gun usually mounted on the wall of a fortress and traversed by means of a swivel (sometimes called a 'swivel gun')

INDEX

A

Amiens, Treaty of, 9
Armit, 1st Lt, 14
Abercromby, Gen, 14
Alcock, Lt RA, 28
Admiralty, 30, 85, 96, 98
Ardagh, 31
Athlone, 65, 70, 73, 87, 94
Aughinish Is, 67
Anchor's Bower, 70
Achill Is, 100

B

Banagher, 16, 70, 72, 73, 76
Baginbun Pt, 16, 74, 101
Ballinamuck, 9
Ballycotton Bay, 85, 105
Ballyvaughan Bay, 67
Bantry Bay, 8, 9, 14, 15, 17, 24, 29, 87, 89, 98
Bantry, Lord, 22
Bantry Town, 15, 16, 18, 22, 25, 26, 82
Battery No.5, 43
Battery No.8, 44
Beckwith, Lt Col, 99, 100
Belvelly, 81
Belvelly Bridge, 82
Belvelly Castle, 82
Berehaven, 17, 24, 26, 30, 31
Bere Is, 17, 24, 25, 26, 29, 31, 48, 51, 74, 76, 87, 89, 92, 96, 97
Birch, Capt RE, 14, 22, 25, 26, 27, 32, 105
Black Head, 67
Boyne, River, 77
Bray Town Commissioners, 42
Brest, 20
British Army Units
    6th (Militia) Bn, Royal Irish Rifles, 79
    20th (East Devonshire) Regt, 2nd Bn, 96
    381 Coast Bty RA, 65
    Connaught Rangers, 17
Bryce, Annan, 22
Buncrana, 85, 95, 96
Burren, The, 67

C

Calder, Adm Sir Robert RN, 15, 24, 98
Cape Colony, 11
Cardew, Capt RE, 14, 105
Carew, Capt RE, 59
Carrickfergus, 8
Carrig Is, 87
Cashla Bay, 68, 76
Castletownbere, 15
Cathcart, Gen Lord, 24, 25, 26, 32, 67, 68, 80
Chace, George, 78
Chatham, Earl of, 14, 26
Ciudadela, 48
Clare, County, 67, 102
Clerk of the Deliveries, 13
Clerk of the Ordnance, 13, 49
Clinton, Col Henry, 25
Clochlan, 27, 29
Coastguard, 36, 38, 40, 41, 47, 105
Coast-watching Service, 17, 104
Cobh, 80
Cochrane, Capt Lord RN, 18
Colinrea Is, 72
Committee of Engineers, 14, 49, 58, 68, 70, 81, 87, 92
Committee on Home Defence, 70
Commissioners of Kingstown Harbour, 38, 47
Commissioners for Limerick Harbour, 96
Commissioners for Wexford Harbour, 75, 76
Cong, 69

Coote, Maj Gen Eyre, 29
Cork, 8, 9, 14, 16, 20, 29, 80, 81, 84, 85, 95, 98, 101
Cork, County, 87, 100, 102
Cornwallis, Gen Lord, 9, 80
Corrib, Lough, 69
Corsica, 9, 11
Cove Is, see Great Is
Cromwell's Castle, 72
Cudmore, Richard, 85

D
Dalkey Sound, 46
D'Arcy, Lt Col Robert RE, 49, 51, 81
DeButts, Capt RE, 105
Defensible Barracks
    Ballinskelligs Bay, 99
    Bolus Head, 99
    Kerry Head, 99
    Rush Pt, 99
Defence Committee, 29, 65
De Forest, Lee, 39
De Galles, Adm Morard, 8
Dingle Peninsula, 99
Donegal, County, 16, 87, 89, 92, 101, 105
Doonaha, 87
Drogheda, 32, 77
Drumanagh, 41
Dublin, 8, 14, 15, 16, 17, 26, 32, 33, 35, 36, 38, 39
    59, 62, 66, 76, 80, 95, 97, 98, 99, 101, 105
Dublin Bay, 38
Dublin United Tramways Co, 48
Dundas, Lt Gen, 14
Dun Laoghaire-Rathdown County, 47, 48, 106
Council
Dunree Head, 49, 53
Dunree Hill, 57
Dunree Military Museum, 57, 58
Dursey Is, 101
Dymchurch, 15
Dyson, Lt RE, 14

E
Eastbourne, 15
Edgar, Mr, 51, 59
Eire, Govt of, 31, 104
Emergency, The, 40, 77, 82, 104

Enoch, Victor, 43
Enniskillen, 15

F
Farrell, Edward, 59, 61
Fenian Brotherhood, 85
Fenian Crisis, 77
Fenian Rebellion, 105
Fenwick, Lt Col RE, 20, 21, 26, 82, 105
Fethard-on-Sea, 16
Finavarra, 67
Fingal County Council, 42
Fisher, Brig Gen Benjamin RE, 14, 21, 26, 29, 32,
    36, 51, 58, 59, 67, 76,, 78, 87, 99, 105
'Flight of the Earls' Heritage Centre, 96
Fort Pt, 74
Fortitude HMS, 9
Forts
    Camden, 8, 80, 81
    Carlisle, 8, 80, 81
    Charles, 8
    Cove, 8
    Down of Inch, 51, 54, 56, 58
    Duncannon, 8, 76, 77
    East (Dunree), 49, 56, 57
    Eliza, 72
    Greencastle, 59, 62, 65, 106
    Ned's Pt, 51, 56
    Pigeon House, 8, 39, 101
    Rathmullen, 51, 56
    Richmond, 77
    West (Knockalla), 49, 51, 53, 54, 56, 57, 58, 61
    Westmoreland, 8, 80
Foyle, Lough, 16, 49, 58, 59, 62, 84, 95, 106
France, 30, 97
Freeman, Brig Gen, 29
Fyers, Maj Gen, 48, 77

G
Galway, 16, 66, 67, 68, 70
Galway Bay, 66, 67, 70, 73, 102
Garinish Is, 16, 18, 21, 22, 25
Garrison Bn, 17
Genealogical Society of Ireland, 47
Glengarriff Harbour, 15, 16, 18, 82
Gogarty, Oliver St John, 47

Great Is, 81, 82, 85
Greencastle, 58, 59, 62

H

Hamline, Lt David RN, 100
Hardwicke, Lord, 24, 74, 97
Hardy, Gen, 9
Hare Is, 67
Haulbowline Is, 81, 84, 95
Hawksbury, Rt Hon Lord, 97
'Hicks' Castle", see 'Towers, Malahide'
Hicks, Frederick, 40
Hoche, 49
Hoche, Gen Lazare, 8
Holloway, Lt Col Sir Charles RE, 22, 23, 24, 25, 26, 81, 82
Hope, Col Alexander, 14
Howth Harbour, 40
Humbert, Gen, 8

I

Illnacullin Garden, 22
Inch Is, 49, 57
Inisheer Is, 102
Inspector General of Fortifications 13, 14, 20, 21, 22, 23, 26, 53, 58, 77, 78, 81, 87
Invalid Bn RA, 36, 38, 56, 95, 96
Irish Civil War, 79
Irish Defence Force, 102

J

James Joyce Museum, 47
Joint Naval & Military Committee, 31
Juno, HMS, 9

K

Keelogue, 70, 72, 73, 87
Kerry, County, 99
Kilcredaun, 87
Kilkerin Pt, 87
Killala Bay, 8, 18
Killiney Bay, 46
King's County, 70, 76
Kingstown, 35, 38
Kinsale, 8, 81, 84
Knockalla Head, 49

L

Lawrence Cove, 24, 27, 28, 29
Lenan Pt, 57
Lewis, Col George RE, 61
Lieutenant General of the Ordnance, 13
Limerick, 8, 14, 87, 95
Lloyd's of London, 102
Lomasney, William Francis, 86
Londonderry, 8, 49, 59
Londonderry, County, 16, 17
Lonehort Pt, 26, 30, 31
Louth, County, 77
Loyal Loughlinstown Yeomanry Gunners, 17
Lyons, James, 85

M

Macamish Pt, 49, 56, 58
Mackay, Capt, see 'Lomasney, William Francis'
Magherees Peninsula, 99
Magilligan Pt, 58, 62, 63, 65
Mahoney, Thomas, 32
Malin Head, 98
Mann, Lt Gen Gother, 20, 49, 58, 62, 76, 81, 87
Marconi Company, The, 39
Marino Pt, 81, 85
Master General of the Ordnance, 21, 26, 70, 95
Meelick, 16, 70, 72, 95
Milligan, Buck, 47
Millmount, The, 77
Minorca, 11, 14, 16, 22, 32, 36, 75
Morse, Lt Gen, 26, 77
Mortella Bay, 9, 11
Mourne's Hill, 70
Mutton Is, 66, 67

N

Naglas Pt, 26
Napoleon, 8, 16, 17, 24, 67, 70, 73, 76, 87
Naval War Signal Stations,
    Bray Head, 102
    Cahermore, 102
    Galley Head, 102
    Loop Head, 102
    Mizen Head, 102
    Sybil Head, 102

Ned's Pt, 49, 56, 57
Nepean, Evan, 26
Newhaven, 67
New Harbour, see 'Newhaven'
Northern Ireland Environment Agency, 67

O

O'Donoghue, Niall, 39, 44
Offaly, County, see 'King's County'
Ordnance, Board of, 13, 14, 16, 17, 18, 23, 24, 25,
    32, 36, 38, 43, 51, 58, 59, 74, 76, 78, 81, 84, 85,
    105

P

Pasley, Gen Sir Charles, 13
Penelope, HMS, 100
Peto, Harold, 22
Piper's Pt, 26
Pole, Rt Hon William Wellesley, 29, 81
Portumna, 95
Preventative Water Guard, 40, 41, 47, 70
Prince of Wales, HMS, 24

Q

Quadrangular Towers
    Bere Is, 89, 92, 96
    Carrig Is, 92
    Doonaha, 89, 92, 96
    Kilcredaun, 92, 94, 96
    Kilkerin, 92, 96
    Ned's Pt, 90, 95, 96
    Rathmullen, 89, 90, 94, 96, 105
    Scattery Is, 89, 92, 94, 96
    Tarbert, 87, 96
Quartermaster General, 26

R

RA & RE Works Committee, 30, 57
Rathmullen, 49, 56
Rathmullen Yeomanry, 17
Redoubts
    Centre (Whiddy Is), 22, 23, 24
    East (Whiddy Is), 22, 23, 24
    Packenham, 87, 92
    West (Bere Is), 26, 29
    West (Whiddy Is), 22, 23, 24

Reenduff Bty, 97
Rerrin, 26, 27, 31
Revenue Service, 36, 75
Ringabella Bay, 85
Ringaskiddy Hill, 81, 85
Rinmore Pt, 66, 67
Rossaveel, 68, 69
Rosslare, 16, 74, 75, 101
Rossleague, 81, 82
Rowley, Lt Col RE, 87
Royal Artillery, 13, 56
Royal Commission on the Defences, 85, 105
of the United Kingdom
Royal Engineers, 13, 14, 25, 43, 104
Royal Engineers in Ireland, 14, 87
Royal Marines, 95, 96
Royal Navy, 80
Royal Sappers & Miners, 13
Royal Staff Corps, 26
Rush Strand, 41

S

Sandycove Bty, 39
Scattery Is, 87
Shanganagh, 43
Sea Fencible District, 100
Shannon, River, 14, 16, 67, 70, 73, 85, 87, 89, 95,
    96
Shannonbridge, 70, 72
Sheffield, Lord, 25
Signal Stations
    Ardmore, 102
    Ballard, 102
    Ballygannon, 99
    Cahore Pt, 99
    Carrigan Head, 101
    Fanad Head, 102
    Kerry Head, 100
    Kilmichael Pt, 99
    Lamcon, 102
    Loop Head, 102
    Malin Head, 101
    Melmore Head, 102
    Mizen Head, 100, 102
    Old Head of Kinsale, 104
    Roberts Head, 100, 102

Sybil Head, 102
  Toe Head, 102
Slieve League Cliffs, 101
Smith, Capt Sir William, 53, 59
South Coast Towers, 16
Spike Is, 8, 80, 81, 84
Stapleton, Capt, 79
Storekeeper General, 13
Surveyor General, 13
Swilly, Lough, 9, 14, 15, 16, 17, 30, 49, 51, 56, 57, 59, 85, 87, 89, 90, 92, 96, 105

T
Tarbert Is, 17, 87, 96
Taylor's Hill, 67
Thurot, Capt, 8
Todd, Lt, 26
Topographical Dictionary of Ireland, 77, 95 (Lewis)
Towers
  Addaya, 32
  Ardagh, 27, 31, 105
  Aughinish, 70, 73
  Baginbun, 74, 75, 76
  Balbriggan, 33, 36, 42, 105
  Balcarrick, 40
  Bartra Rock, see 'Bullock'
  Belvelly, 81, 82
  Bray Head, 36
  Bray Pt, 42
  Bullock, 35, 36, 46
  Cashla Bay, 69, 70
  Cathcart, 27, 28, 29, 31, 48
  Clochlan, 27, 31
  Corke Abbey, 34, 42
  Dalkey Is, 33, 35, 36, 38, 39, 46, 51
  Drumanagh, 36, 40
  Dun Laoghaire Harbour, 36, 47
  Fanesker, 72, 73
  Finavarra, 70, 73
  Fort Pt, 74, 75, 76
  Garinish, 18, 21, 82
  Glasthule, 36, 38, 47
  Greencastle, 59, 61, 84, 92
  Haulbowline, 82, 84, 85
  Howth Hill, 33, 36, 39

  Inch Is, 54
  Ireland's Eye, 33, 34, 36, 39
  Knockalla, 54
  Loughlinstown, 36, 43
  Macamish, 53, 58
  Maghera Pt, 36, 43
  Magilligan , 17, 59, 65, 106
  Malahide, 33, 40, ,105
  Manly, 27, 29, 30, 31
  Manning, 85
  Meelick, 73
  Mount Park, see 'Bray Pt'
  Portmarnock, 40
  Portrane, 33, 36, 38, 40
  Red Is, 33, 36, 39, 42
  Ringaskiddy, 82, 84, 85, 86
  Roche's Pt, 81
  Rossleague, 82, 83, 85, 86
  Rush, 33, 36, 39, 40
  Sandycove, 35, 36, ,38, 39, 46
  Sandymount, 35, 36, 48
  Santandria, 13, 28
  Seapoint, 47
  Shenick's Is, 33, 41
  Sutton, 33
  Tara Hill, 38, 39, 43, 106
  Williamstown, 34, 35, 36, 43, 47
Trinidad, 11
Trotter, Brig Gen, 18
Twiss, Brig Gen William, 14, 15, 18, 22, 32, 49, 76, 80

U
'Ulysses' (James Joyce), 47
Union, Irish Acts of, 13, 14
United States of America, 16, 81, 102

V
Vallencey, Maj Gen Charles, 14, 87
Veteran Bn, 17
Vintage Radio Museum, 39

W
Wakefield, Edmund, 100
War Office, 29, 31, 40, 47, 105

Warren, Commodore Sir John RN, 49
Waterford City, 8, 14, 76
Waterford, County, 102
Wellesley, Sir Arthur, 29, 74, 75
Western Pilots, 96
Westmacott, Lt Col, 22
Wexford, 16, 32, 74, 76, 99
Whiddy Is, 15, 16, 18, 22, 24, 25
Whitshed, Rear Adm RN, 32, 98, 101
Wickham, Rt Hon William, 24, 32
Woolwich, 56, 57
Works, Board of, 38
Wray, Col, 29
Wright, Capt George RE, 78, 105

Y
Yeomanry Corps, 77
York, Duke of, 14, 67
Yorke, Rt Hon Charles, 24
Youghal, 105